D1558029

Take Two Tablets ...and Call Moses!

Quick Bible Lessons to Pick Up 'n' Do!
Elementary Lessons

**Edited by Lois Keffer
and Mary Grace Becker**

NEXGEN®

Building the New Generation of Believers

An Imprint of Cook Communications Ministries
Colorado Springs, Colorado

Just Add Kids: Take Two Tablets and Call Moses!
Copyright © 2004 Cook Communications Ministries

Scripture quotations, unless otherwise noted, are from

THE HOLY BIBLE, NEW INTERNATIONAL VERSION (NIV)
Copyright © 1973, 1978, 1984 by International Bible Society.
Used by permission of Zondervan Publishing House. All rights reserved.

Edited by: Mary Grace Becker, Lois Keffer
Written by: Debbie Allmon, Mary Grace Becker, Kathleen Dowdy, Faye Spieker, Susan Epperson, Paula Frost, Kim Gunderson, Lois Keffer, Kathy Link, Shirley Francis
Art Direction: Nancy L. Haskins
Cover Design: Helen Harrison
Interior Design: Nancy L. Haskins, Helen Harrison, Lois Keffer
Illustrators: Kris and Sharon Cartwright and Lois Keffer

Printed in the United States

First printing, 2004
1 2 3 4 5 6 7 8 9 10   06 05 04

ISBN 078144067x

Table of Contents

Quick Start Guide

Just Add Kids! elementary lessons give your kids great Bible teaching and serious discipleship without hours of preparation. You and your kids will love these large group/small group lessons. Two options let you take the lesson from super simple to more challenging.

If you're looking for an "instant" lesson that you can pick up and do at the last minute, you've got it in Bible 4U! and Shepherd's Spot.

All you need is a photocopier and basic classroom supplies such as pencils, scissors and glue sticks. Copy the **Bible 4U!** instant drama and the **Shepherd's Spot** handout and you're ready to go.

Are you looking for something beyond the basics?

The optional **Get Set** section of the lessons gives you an opportunity to get a puppet into the action. "Schooner" is a mouthy macaw whose bright remarks will bring giggles and grins each week. And he does a smack-up job of setting up the Bible story.

Don't have a puppet ministry team in your church? How about recruiting middle schoolers? The lively back and forth between Schooner and the Leader is right up their alley. What a great way to get them involved in ministry to younger children!

Now for the heart of the lesson

Bible 4U!

The Bible is full of drama! What better way to teach than with fascinating dramas that take a unique approach to each Bible story? Photocopy the instant drama, pull volunteers from your group to read the roles and you're ready to go.

You'll keep your knowledgeable students engaged, and give kids who are new to God's Word a solid foundation of Biblical truth. The dramas call for just a few characters. You may want to play the main role yourself. Or, call on a teen or adult drama troupe to prepare and present the dramas each week. Either way, kids will see the Bible stories come to life in unforgettable ways.

1.
Bible 4U!

Shepherd's Spot

This is the second essential step of the lesson. After **Bible 4U!**, kids break into small groups with one adult helper for every eight to ten kids. Nothing leaves a more indelible impact on kids' lives than the warm, personal touch of a caring adult. The photocopiable instructions and handouts will give your helpers the confidence they need to help kids consider how to live out what they've learned.

In the **Shepherd's Spot**, kids will read the story straight from the Bible. They'll learn basic Bible skills, and complete a fun, photocopiable handout that helps them understand how to get the story off the page and into their lives. They'll close each week by sharing concerns and praying together.

2.
Shepherd's
Spot

Workshop Wonders

And there's more! Each week, the optional **Workshop Wonders** section gives you a game, craft, science or cooking activity that gets your kids out of their chairs and into the action.

The **Workshop Wonders** activities require more than the usual classroom supplies. If you choose one of these activities, you'll need to pick up cooking or science ingredients or a few simple craft or game supplies. If you don't mind a little extra preparation, you'll find that there's nothing like a little hands-on action to bring that moment of learning wonder to kids' faces.

These special activities are guaranteed to make a memory and help the Bible lesson stick with kids for a long time to come.

That's it! You can go for a quick, simple lesson with **Bible 4U!** and the **Shepherd's Spot**.

If you wish, add another level of excitement and learning with the Schooner script in the optional **Get Set** section of each lesson.

And if you love teaching with activities, do a little shopping and give kids the memorable experiences of **Workshop Wonders**.

Do you want to give your kids even more great stuff?

How About Staff?

Finding Schooner

If you do the **Get Set** option to open the lessons, you'll need to purchase a parrot or scarlet macaw puppet.

You'll find a great selection on the Internet, in all sizes and prices. Type "scarlet macaw puppet" into your favorite search engine and browse until you find the puppet that suits your price range.

You need just a few helpers to make Just Add Kids lessons a great experience for you and your kids!

1. A leader/emcee hosts the **Bible 4U!** instant drama each week. For a quick presentation, pull kids from your group to read the roles in the dramas. When there are just one or two parts, you may want to step into the leading role yourself.

2. You may wish to ask a small drama troupe to prepare the stories each week. Five or six volunteers who serve on a rotating basis can easily cover the stories with just a few minutes' preparation.

3. For the **Shepherd's Spot**, you'll need one adult leader for every eight to ten kids. You'll need caring adults in this role—people who are good listeners and feel comfortable sharing their lives with kids. This is a great first step into children's ministry for adults who haven't taught before.

4. If you choose to do the optional **Get Set** puppet script, you'll need a leader and a puppeteer. It's best to use the same leader who hosts the Bible dramas. If you recruit a couple of people to play Schooner, they can rotate every few weeks.

For Overachievers

Do you have a great stage set-up at your church? Then you may want to go for some flash and glitz. Give Schooner a little tropical cabana with a palm tree and a sea-breezy backdrop. Make sure your leader has an obnoxious tropical shirt to slip on.

Don't forget the music! Warm kids up each week with lively, interactive praise songs. Then bring on Schooner's set to the tune of island rhythms.

Equip your drama troupe with a box full of Bibletime costumes. You'll find tips for props and staging in the "for Overachievers" box just before each Bible story. Of course, all this pizzazz is purely optional. The most important ingredient in a wonderful Bible lesson is YOU—the warm, caring leader whose love for kids calls you into children's ministry in the first place! There is absolutely no substitute for the personal attention you give to children each week. You become the model of Jesus himself through your gifts of time and commitment.

God bless you as you minister to his kids!

Baby in a Basket

Get Set
LARGE GROUP ■ Greet kids and do a puppet skit. Schooner finds out about God's care for a baby named Moses.

❏ large bird puppet ❏ puppeteer

Bible 4U! Instant Drama
LARGE GROUP ■ Aaron tells how hard it was to hide baby Moses and how God guided the baby as he floated down the river in his own little basket boat.

❏ 6 actors ❏ jacket or blanket ❏ copies of pp. 10–11, *Everybody Loves Moses* script ❏ 4 numbered balls ❏ bag

Shepherd's Spot
SMALL GROUP ■ Create a paper pop-up of Moses' basket floating in the river. Pull out the baby and find an important message! Share concerns and pray together. Send home the Special Delivery handout.

❏ Bibles ❏ pencils ❏ scissors ❏ glue sticks ❏ copies of p. 14, *Float Your Boat!* ❏ copies of p. 16, *Special Delivery*

Workshop Wonders
SMALL GROUP ■ Like the basket used to carry baby Moses, a woven bag will carry and help protect the things your kids care about.

❏ colored burlap ❏ colored sticky tape ❏ multi-colored yarn ❏ scissors ❏ plastic sewing needles

---

Bible Basis
The birth of Moses. Exodus 1:12–16, 2:1–10

Learn It!
God takes care of his own.

Live It!
Trust God to take care of you.

Bible Verse
May the God of hope fill you with all joy and peace as you trust in him. Romans 15:13

Neighbor: What's with all the noise over here? Did I hear a baby crying?

Miriam: A baby? Why would we have a baby? That was, um…Aaron. He was crying because I wouldn't let him have a bagel.

Aaron rolls his eyes and shakes his head.

Neighbor: Aaron, aren't you a little old for tantrums?

Aaron: I guess I am. I'll try to do better.

Neighbor exits.

All: Phew!

Aaron: Thanks, Miriam. I owe you one. *(Sniffs air.)* Pee-yu!

Moses begins crying.

Mother: He needs his diaper changed and here comes our neighbor again.

Mother and baby hide. Crying stops.

Neighbor: Now who's crying?

Aaron: Oh…um… that was me again. My stomach hurts. I had lentils for lunch and they always leave me feeling a little, um, bloated.

Neighbor: *(Sniffs)* What's that awful smell?

Aaron: Oh, sorry. It must have been those lentils.

Neighbor: Who needs such noisy, smelly neighbors? I have all the luck. *(Exits.)*

Aaron: Boy, was that embarrassing. *(He takes Moses.)* Come here, little Moses. You sure are a lot of trouble. But you're pretty cute. *(Tickles the baby.)* Gitchie, gitchie, goo! *(Moses giggles and babble.)*

Aaron: Shhhh! Stuff it, kid. You're being way too loud.

Miriam: Way to go, Aaron. Here comes the neighbor again.

Mother and baby hide, as neighbor enters.

Neighbor: Okay. I know I hear a baby.

Aaron: Oh, you must have heard Miriam and me. We were…singing. *(Sings loudly.)* Gaga, goo-goo, yabadaba do!

Miriam joins in singing nonsense.

Neighbor: Your family is just plain crazy—did you know that? *(Exits.)*

Family exits. Aaron comes to the front.

Aaron: Well, you get the idea. That lasted for three months! Every minute we were afraid an Egyptian soldier would come bursting in. It was scary.

One night when I couldn't sleep, I looked around and saw my Mother working in the moonlight. *(Mother enters kneels and mimes lining basket.)* It looked like she had a basket. I could tell from the icky smell that she was lining the basket with black gooey stuff called pitch. I got up to find out what was going on. *(Steps back and speaks to Mother in a stage whisper.)* Mom, what's the deal?

Mother: I have a plan. I believe God will take care of Moses! *(Exits.)*

Aaron: She had a plan, all right. It all depended on God's protection.

Enter Miriam, she pantomimes action.

Miriam went to the river with Moses in the basket. She put the basket into the river and watched it float away. It was a heart-stopping moment. What if water got into the basket and it sank? What if Egyptian soldiers found it? What if there were hungry crocodiles? But none of those things happened. God watched over my baby brother and the basket floated into the reeds where the princess was bathing. Pharaoh's daughter found him! *(Enter princess.)* She picked him out of the water and decided to keep him. Then Miriam rushed over and asked…

Miriam: Shall I go and get one of the Hebrew women to nurse the baby for you?

Princess: Yes, go *(Princess looks adoringly at baby until Miriam returns with the mother.)* Take this baby and nurse him for me. I will pay you. *(They exit.)*

Aaron: So that's how Moses ended up back home—safe, this time. When he's older we'll take him back to the princess and he'll grow up in the palace. The way I figure it, God must have a special plan for this little boy! Oh, man, he just spit up on my blanket!

Well, doesn't that story just float your boat! Heads up—I've got some questions coming your way.

Toss the four numbered balls to different parts of the room. Bring the kids with the balls to the front one by one and ask these questions. Allow kids to get help from the group if they need it. After each correct answer, let kids drop the ball into a bag.

 ■ **Why did Moses' family have to hide him?**

 ■ **What do you think of his mother's idea to set him afloat on the river?**

 ■ **Suppose you were Moses' older (sister/brother). What would you have thought as you watched his little basket float away?**

 ■ **Tell about a time when God took care of you.**

Putting a baby in a basket and setting it afloat in a river is a pretty radical idea. It's a huge risk. But when you stop to think about it, it's a very small thing for our God to guide that basket right where he wanted it to go. Moses' mother didn't think only about the risks. She thought about God. She remembered that he's powerful and loving and that he promises to take care of those who love him.

Bible Verse
May the God of hope fill you with all joy and peace as you trust in him.
Romans 15:13

So here's the situation. Egypt is full of soldiers who are ready to kill any Hebrew baby boy they can find. The current of the river is strong. The basket is made to be waterproof, but will it really float? In the face of all these risks, Moses' mother trusted in God's care. She believed that God was more powerful than the soldiers, in control of the river, and that—more than anything—he loved her child very much. God didn't disappoint her. Things couldn't have turned out better!

Pharaoh was one of the meanest people on earth, but God didn't let that get in the way of plans to make Moses a mighty leader. God cares for you in the same way. Honest! No ruler, no power of nature, no mean soldiers can stop God from caring for you, so trust him! Today in your shepherd groups you'll learn more about trusting God.

Dismiss kids to their shepherd groups.

2 Shepherd's Spot.

Gather your small group and help kids find Exodus 1 in their Bibles. The Bible is lots of little books inside one book. There are sixty-six little books, in fact, and Exodus is the second one.

Exodus tells about God's people who were slaves to Pharaoh, the mean king of Egypt. Their lives were hard. But God had a plan, and it started with a baby boy who would grow up to be a great leader. The bad news was that Hebrew baby boys were supposed to be killed. So Moses' mother made him a special basket and set him afloat in the river.

■ What would it be like to watch your baby float away on a big river?

Moses' mother trusted God completely. And God guided Moses' basket right into the hands of a princess who raised him as her own son. You know what? God cares for you in that very same way.

■ Who can think of something that would make you feel hopeless?

God wants us to trust him. He has ways of working things out that we could never even dream of! Let's make a floating basket that reminds us to keep our hope in God.

Pass out copies of "Float Your Boat." You may want to use a craft knife to open the slit in the basket. Have kids add their names to the Bible verse, then follow the assembly instructions on the handout.

Float Your Boat!

1. Cut out both pieces on the heavy lines.
2. Cut the slit in the basket.
3. Write your name on the blank in the middle of the Bible verse.
4. Fold the long piece in half.
5. Fold the bottom flaps out to form a stand.
6. Fold the lid piece in half and push it through the slit.
7. "Open" the basket and pull out the baby!

Trust God to take care of you, just as he took care of baby Moses.

May the God of hope fill you, with all joy and peace as you trust in him. Romans 15:13

Let trust in God float your boat!

14 Permission to photocopy this script granted for local church use. Copyright © Cook Communications Ministries. Printed in Just Add Kids Lessons on Jesus 4U.

■ What does trusting God look like in your life?

Let's start trusting God right now by praying about things that worry us. Encourage kids to share prayer requests, then close with prayer. Dear Lord, it's amazing how you took care of baby Moses. Help us to trust you to care for us in the same way. We pray for (mention each child's requests). We ask you to fill all our hearts with joy and peace. In Jesus' name, amen.

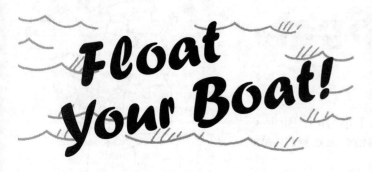

Float Your Boat!

1. Cut out both pieces on the heavy lines.
2. Cut the slit in the basket.
3. Write your name on the blank in the middle of the Bible verse.
4. Fold the long piece in half.
5. Fold the bottom flaps out to form a stand.
6. Fold the lid piece in half and push it through the slit.
7. "Open" the basket and pull out the baby!

Trust God to take care of you, just as he took care of baby Moses.

May the God of hope fill you,

with all joy and peace as you trust in him.
Romans 15:13

Let trust in God float your boat!

Workshop Wonders

Get List:
- ❏ colored burlap (found at fabric and discount stores)
- ❏ colored sticky tape
- ❏ multi-colored yarn
- ❏ scissors
- ❏ children's plastic sewing needles

Just as the woven basket protected and carried baby Moses to safety in today's story, your kids will make a burlap pouch bag to carry and protect the things they care about. Before class, cut rectangles of burlap (32 in. x 11 in.) to form the bags. Cut 24 in. x 2 in. burlap strips for the shoulder straps.

Moses became a powerful leader, but when he was born he was as tiny and helpless as any other baby. How easy it would have been for the Egyptians to find him and kill him. But God protected baby Moses. Moses' mother placed little Moses in a basket and sent him on his way down the Nile River to eventually be scooped up by Pharaoh's daughter. God used this little journey on the river to place Moses where he needed to be, right in the middle of a royal household. Amazing!

- ■ **Who took care of you when you were a baby? Let's take a moment to praise God for watching over us just as he did for Moses.**
- ■ **Do babies know when danger is upon them? What is your first reaction when you're afraid or in danger?**

It gives me a lot of comfort to know we have a God who cares. God used a basket to protect Moses from the chilly waters and the creepy-crawlies that called the Nile River home. Let's make our own basket bag to protect our special things. It will be a great place to keep papers, drawings or even your Bible. Let it remind you of baby Moses' basket boat and that God cares about us just as he cared for Moses.

- ■ **On a scale of 1-5 how do you rate your trust in God when you're afraid or too weak to help yourself? Why that number?**

Distribute the burlap pieces. Have kids fold over the larger rectangular piece leaving 4-inches at one end exposed. This 4-inch piece will form the flap for the bag. Use the colored sticky tape to join the two burlap sides. Finish taping all the raw edges.

- ■ **Share a time your family experienced God's protection—maybe it was when you were on a trip or maybe it was something that happened when you were at home.**

- ■ **Besides physical danger, what other things can make us afraid and in need of God's care?**

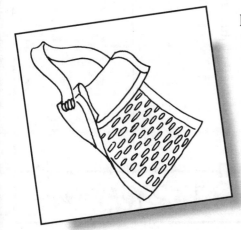

Help kids thread yarn into the large, plastic needles. Starting at the bottom of the bag, embroider rows of yarn in an "in and out" weave pattern across the front of the bag. Kids can put one hand inside the bag as they sew. To finish the bag, whip stitch the ends of the burlap strip to the backside for a shoulder strap or handle.

God protects and cares even when we are unaware—much like he did for one giggly, wiggly baby named Moses. Trust him!

Fold down the corners to start your paper airplane.

SPECIAL DELIVERY

"How can a simple faith (much like the faith a toddler has in Mom and Dad) help you place your trust in God?

Today at church we heard how God protected baby Moses.

TO

Trust God to take care of you.

Open the Bible to Exodus 1:12–16, 2:1–10 and read about God's lifesaving plan for little Moses. Then make quick and easy bread "baskets" for your family to enjoy. In a bowl mix 1/3 c. of cream cheese with 1 Tbsp. chopped walnuts and 1 Tbsp. crushed pineapple. Spread the mixture on a warm and toasty whole wheat English muffin. Roll up a ham slice; place it in the middle. Fold the muffin in half and take a bite! As you make more breadbaskets remember that God takes care of his own.

Bible Verse

May the God of hope fill you with all joy and peace as you trust in him.
Romans 15:13

◇ When is it easy to trust God? When is it hard?

◇ Is there something that's frightening to you? How can you trust God to take care of it?

☆ Family FUN

Live It! ☆

"Moses! Moses!"

Get Set
LARGE GROUP ■ Greet kids and do a puppet skit. Schooner learns that when God speaks, bushes snap, crackle and pop!

❏ *large bird puppet* ❏ *puppeteer*

Bible 4U! Instant Drama
LARGE GROUP ■ Bernie Bush and Stony Ground tell about their experiences the day God called Moses to go back to Egypt.

❏ *two actors* ❏ *copies of pp. 20–21, Hunka Hunka Burnin' Bush script*
❏ *4 numbered balls* ❏ *bag*

Shepherd's Spot
SMALL GROUP ■ Create a 3D burning bush as a reminder to listen for God. Share concerns and pray together. Send home the Special Delivery handout.

❏ *Bibles* ❏ *pencils* ❏ *glue sticks* ❏ *copies of p. 24, Listen Up!* ❏ *copies of p. 26, Special Delivery*

Workshop Wonders
SMALL GROUP ■ Make a sparkling bush in a bottle as you review today's Bible story.

❏ *bottled water* ❏ *light corn syrup* ❏ *red and orange shiny confetti* ❏ *evergreen branches or plant cuttings* ❏ *pitcher* ❏ *funnel* ❏ *tablecloth*

Bible Basis
Moses and the burning bush
Exodus 3:1–14

Learn It!
God speaks to us.

Live It!
Listen for God.

Bible Verse
Show me your ways, O LORD, teach me your paths.
Psalm 25:4

Quick Takes

Exodus 3:1–14

Now Moses was tending the flock of Jethro his father-in-law, the priest of Midian, and he led the flock to the far side of the desert and came to Horeb, the mountain of God.

2 There the angel of the Lord appeared to him in flames of fire from within a bush. Moses saw that though the bush was on fire it did not burn up.

3 So Moses thought, "I will go over and see this strange sight— why the bush does not burn up."

4 When the Lord saw that he had gone over to look, God called to him from within the bush, "Moses! Moses!" And Moses said, "Here I am."

5 "Do not come any closer," God said. "Take off your sandals, for the place where you are standing is holy ground."

6 Then he said, "I am the God of your father, the God of Abraham, the God of Isaac and the God of Jacob." At this, Moses hid his face, because he was afraid to look at God.

7 The Lord said, "I have indeed seen the misery of my people in Egypt. I have heard them crying out because of their slave drivers, and I am concerned about their suffering.

8 So I have come down to rescue them from the hand of the Egyptians and to bring them up out of that land into a good and spacious land, a land flowing with milk and honey—the home of the Canaanites, Hittites, Amorites, Perizzites, Hivites and Jebusites.

9 And now the cry of the Israelites has reached me, and I have seen the way the Egyptians are oppressing them.

10 So now, go. I am sending you to Pharaoh to bring my people the Israelites out of Egypt."

11 But Moses said to God, "Who am I, that I should go to Pharaoh and bring the Israelites out of Egypt?"

12 And God said, "I will be with you. And this will be the sign to you that it is I who have sent you: When you have brought the people out of Egypt, you will worship God on this mountain."

13 Moses said to God, "Suppose I go to the Israelites and say to them, 'The God of your fathers has sent me to you,' and they ask me, 'What is his name?' Then what shall I tell them?"

14 God said to Moses, "I AM WHO I AM. This is what you are to say to the Israelites: 'I AM has sent me to you.'"

Insights

As the baby boy rescued by Pharaoh's daughter grew to be a man, he saw what was happening to his people. Though he enjoyed princely privileges, he couldn't ignore how his people suffered. One day he went to watch them hard at work. Rage and heartbreak tore at Moses as his people groaned under cruel Egyptian taskmasters.

When Moses saw an Egyptian beating a Hebrew slave, he snapped. Thinking no one was watching Moses killed the Egyptian and hid his body in the sand. The next day he discovered that the slaves knew of his crime, and so did Pharaoh. So Moses ran for his life.

He crossed the Sinai Peninsula, went north around the Gulf of Aqaba, then south to the land of Midian, about 200 miles southeast of Egypt. There he married, raised two sons and lived for forty years in obscurity as a common shepherd. God brought an end to these quiet years of exile when he spoke to Moses on the barren, rocky slopes of Mount Sinai.

God commissioned Moses to return to Egypt and set the Israelites free.

Moses and God had quite a conversation! You'd practically have to pull today's children out of the world of TV and video games and onto a desert mountainside to give them space to hear God speak. God used miraculous "special effects" to get Moses' attention.

What would it take for your kids? Perhaps the gentle attention of an adult who's dedicated to opening their eyes to the wondrous love of their Creator. A teacher who's heard God speak in his or her life and is willing to give witness to the experience. Use this lesson to help kids understand that the mighty maker of the universe speaks to his people, and it is our privilege to listen and obey.

 **Get Set** ∙∙∙

It's great to see you. We're going to have a "hot time" today complete with flames in the desert and a bush that was on fire but didn't burn up. And Moses saw it all. Schooner, join me and say hello to the group. *Schooner pops up*

Leader: Say hello, Schooner.

Schooner: *(preoccupied.)* Hello, Schooner.

Leader: No, no. Say hello to the group.

Schooner: Hello, group…

Leader: Are you feeling well, Schooner?

Schooner: Huh?

Leader: Are you feeling well?

Schooner: *(pensive again)*

Leader: Do you have a temperature?

Schooner: Hmm?

Leader: Maybe I should just clean your ears.

Schooner: What?

Leader: *(hold nose)* Earth to Schooner. Come in, Schooner.

Schooner: Sorry, boss. I was just thinking.

Leader: About?

Schooner: About what you said.

Leader: Remind me, please. It's been awhile!

Schooner: A fiery bush that doesn't burn.

Leader: Of course. Today's Bible story. Pretty amazing stuff.

Schooner: It reminds me of a time…

Leader: Yes?

Schooner: …when I was just a cute little ball of feathers.

Leader: Go on.

Schooner: And I saw my very first campfire.

Leader: A campfire!

Schooner: The campers used leaves, branches, dried bush twigs to build an awesome fire.

Leader: All those things would make a fire burn bright.

Schooner: That's what I don't get, boss. A bush on fire always burns.

Leader: Of course.

Schooner: Was Moses sure the bush was really on fire?

Leader: Yup. Flames of fire, the Bible says.

Schooner: Well then, did Moses remember to bring the marshmallows?

Leader: Uh…no.

Schooner: Hot dogs?

Leader: No…no.

Schooner: Did Moses try to put it out?

Leader: No, Schooner. God was speaking through the bush.

Schooner: Amazing times two!

Leader: I agree. In today's story, God does his best to get Moses' attention.

Schooner: God is full of surprises.

Leader: And a curious Moses took a look!

Schooner: I would too. *Squawk!*

Leader: What God had to say to Moses was pretty important.

Schooner: How cool…I mean hot…I mean cool that God Almighty, the King of the Universe stopped to have a chat with Moses.

Leader: God uses people to accomplish his plans, Schooner.

Schooner: Does God talk to people today?

Leader: Most certainly.

Schooner: To children too?

Leader: God speaks to everyone…through his Word, moms and dads, teachers and those with a heart for his holy ways.

Schooner: What does God sound like?

Leader: Well, sometimes he speaks in unexpected ways like the burning bush. Sometimes he speaks through his Word, and sometimes through whispers in our hearts.

Schooner: I'll be on the listen for God. After all, listening is a big part of my job.

Leader: I never would have guessed! Bible 4U! up next.

1 Bible 4U!

Welcome to Bible 4U! Theater. We have a really hot topic today. Two fiery guests are going to tell us an explosive story about a hot time in the ol' desert—a time when God spoke to a man and great prophet named Moses.

You may remember Moses as the baby whose mother floated him in a basket on the Nile River so he wouldn't be found and killed by Egyptian soldiers.

Instant Prep
Before class, ask two volunteer readers to play the roles of Bernie Bush and Stony Ground. Give them copies of the "Hunka, Hunka Burning Bush" script below to review. Stony Ground sits cross-legged in front of Bernie Bush who stands as they read the story.

Moses grew up as a prince, but he saw how difficult life was for his family and the other Hebrew slaves. One day he killed a man who was beating a slave. Then he ran for his life! He couldn't go back to Egypt because he was a wanted man. So he lived as a shepherd in the desert in a country called Midian. He raised a family, tended his sheep, and minded his own business...until he got a wake-up call from God.

It started off like any other day. Then, all of a sudden...but wait! I don't want to give the story away. You've got a ringside seat and we're hot on the trail of hearing how God kept one man on the right path!

for Overachievers
Have a two-person drama team prepare the story. Dress Bernie Bush in a green camouflage shirt with strips of yellow and orange cellophane taped to the collar and arms. Wrap Stony Ground in a large piece of burlap. Prepare a backdrop of desert mountain scenery.

Hunka Hunka Burnin' Bush
Based on Exodus 3:1–14

Bernie and Stony enter.

Bernie Bush: Ladies and gentlemen! I'm the famous Bernie Bush. And this *(gestures to Stony)* is my faithful partner, Stony Ground. Stony and I have been together for years.

Stony Ground: I'm not any old stony ground. No sirree, I'm the very ground Moses stood on when God spoke to him.

Bernie Bush: It started just like any other day in the desert—hot, dry and dusty. The only sound was the hungry bleating of the flock of sheep that Moses was tending. Then, all of sudden, I had a really strange feeling!

Stony Ground: I'll say. You looked like you were about to burst.

Bernie Bush: And that's exactly what I did. I burst into flames!

Stony Ground: Oh, man, you were on fire!

Bernie Bush: Being on fire is usually a pretty bad thing for a bush. But I didn't feel hot at all. Instead, there was this awesome warmth that actually felt good. Then I noticed Moses staring at me in amazement. There I was in all my blazing glory, but not burning up. He started toward me to get a better look.

Stony Ground: And just as I was thinking things could not get any weirder, a voice came from the flames. *(in a deep voice)* "MOSES! MOSES!"

Bernie Bush: *(looking around)* It felt like that voice came from me, but I knew it wasn't me doing the talking.

Stony Ground: *(snorts with laughter)* Moses didn't have any problem with talking bushes. He just said, " Here I am," right back to Bernie.

Bernie Bush: But then God let us all know who was really doing the talking!

Stony Ground: *(chest swells with pride)* Oh, yeah! This is the best part! God told Moses to take off his sandals 'cuz he was standing on holy ground. Man, ever since I can remember I've been treated like dirt. But the presence of God changed me to holy ground!

Bernie Bush: Boy, God's words lit a fire under Moses! He couldn't yank those sandals off fast enough!

Stony Ground: Then God spoke again. *(in a deep voice)* "I am the God of your ancestors, the God of Abraham, Isaac and Jacob."

Bernie Bush: Whoa! Moses hid his face and was afraid to even look at me.

Stony Ground: *(with a tremor in his voice)* Moses was shaking so much, the earth beneath his feet trembled. I ought to know—I was the earth beneath his feet!

Bernie Bush: God gave Moses a mission—to go back to Egypt and talk Pharaoh into letting the Hebrew slaves leave.

Stony Ground: You'd think Moses would have realized that if God can light a fire under Bernie without burning him up, he can do anything. But no, Moses was looking for the fire escape.

Bernie Bush: Moses tried to talk God into finding a better leader. He had excuse after excuse.

Stony Ground: But God fired back, "I will be with you."

Bernie Bush: So Moses asked God "What if I tell them the God of our fathers sent me and they ask me 'what is his name?'"

Stony Ground: I wondered if God was going to turn Moses into toast. Not very many people talk back to the God of all creation!

Bernie Bush: I think it's cool to know that God talks to us and that he answers our questions!

Stony Ground: You're one to be talking about being cool—you were flamin'!

Bernie Bush: Anyway, God didn't beat around the bush!

Stony Ground: *(rolling his eyes)* Oh, man, that's bad!

Bernie Bush: Didn't you love the way God answered Moses' questions?

Stony Ground: *(in a deep voice)* "I AM who I am—tell the Israelites: I AM has sent you."

Bernie Bush: And believe me, when the great I AM spoke Moses listened, Stony worshiped and my ears burned, my heart burned. As a matter of fact, I was one hunka, hunka burnin' bush!

Stony Ground: Moses got the message. And with a little help from his brother and the miracles God gave him to do, he eventually got the job done.

Bernie Bush: Whoever thought we'd be part of a scene like that? I mean, I'm just a bush in the desert, and you're just, well…rocky ground.

Stony Ground: God can do the most amazing things with plain old people and things.

Bernie Bush: I guess we got our fifteen minutes of fame, didn't we?

Stony Ground: You bet! We were witnesses to history.

Let's hear it for Bernie and Stony, an amazing couple of guys! Now let's have some fun and see how well their story stuck!

Toss the four numbered balls to different parts of the room. Bring the kids with the balls to the front one by one and ask these questions. Allow kids to get help from the group if they need it. After each correct answer, let kids drop the ball into a bag.

■ As Moses was tending his sheep in the desert, what caught his eye?

■ What was the message God had for Moses?

■ So after this happens Moses goes back to his family. What does he tell his wife?

■ Do you think God talks to people today? Explain.

If you wish, toss out small wrapped candies when all the balls are in the bag.

This was quite a shocker for Moses. And I don't mean just the part about the bush being on fire without burning up. You see, Moses had run away from Egypt forty years before this happened. He seemed to enjoy his peaceful life as a shepherd. Then—BOOM!—God speaks to him and changes everything. Now he has to go back to Egypt and deal with nasty old Pharaoh. He knows the news he has to deliver isn't what Pharaoh wants to hear. But there's no doubt about it, God's directions were loud and clear.

Bible Verse
Show me your way, O LORD,
teach me your paths.
Psalm 25:4

Has God ever spoken to you in a surprising way? Maybe an idea about how to help someone suddenly popped into your head. Maybe you suddenly felt that you needed to pray about something. Maybe words from the Bible just popped off the page and you understood, "This is for YOU!"

Today in your shepherd groups you'll discover more about how God speaks to us today.

Dismiss kids to their shepherd groups.

2 Shepherd's Spot

Gather your small group and help kids find Exodus 3 in their Bibles.

- ■ **Who remembers where to find Exodus?**

- ■ **Any guesses about what the word "Exodus" means?**

It means "exit." The Hebrew slaves needed a strong leader to help them get out of Egypt. God chose Moses for the job.

Have volunteers take turns reading Exodus 3:1-14 aloud.

When God spoke to Moses, it wasn't just a friendly chat. God had marching orders: go back to Egypt and tell Pharaoh to set my people free. Moses kept thinking of good reasons not to go. But God kept coming back with answers.

- ■ **Have you ever had a conversation with God? What was that like?**
- ■ **Do you think God likes to talk to us? Explain.**

Sometimes at school or at home you have to work really hard to get someone's attention. It's not like that with God. He's always paying attention, and he has important things to say.

Hand out copies of "Listen Up!" (p. 24). **We don't usually play with fire in the classroom, but today is an exception. Our burning bush handout is a great reminder to listen to what God has to say.**

Help kids cut out and assemble burning bush according to the instructions on the handout. Invite a volunteer to read the Bible verse that runs around the top of the bush. **See the bottom section there under the bush? You get to mark how you'll listen for God, then sign your name.**

Invite kids to share their prayer concerns, then close with prayer. **Dear Lord, thank you for being a God who listens to our concerns and speaks to our hearts. Today we pray for** (mention each child's name and prayer requests). **Father, we ask that you'll give us listening hearts. Help us to be quiet and open to what you have to say to us. In Jesus name, amen.**

Listen Up!

God used a burning bush to get Moses' attention. God still has important things to say to people who take time to listen.

Use this model of the burning bush to help you remember to listen for God's voice every day.

1. Cut out the bush and the fire.

2. Fill out the box at the bottom of the bush. Then fold it back and glue it to the back of the bush.

3. Fold the fire piece back on both dotted lines.

4. Glue the back tab of the fire to the space marked at the bottom of the bush.

Show me your way, O Lord, teach me your paths.

Psalm 25:4

Glue fire tab here.

Signed _____

___ I'll find time to be quiet and think about God.

___ I'll pray "listening prayers."

___ I'll read his Word.

God's voice?

listening hearts. How will you listen for

God still speaks to people who have

God speaks.
Have a listen!

Fold back and glue to bush.

God speaks.
Have a listen!

Cover your work table with the tablecloth.

Imagine the shepherd Moses quietly tending his sheep as we heard in today's Bible story. It's the same job he'd done day in and day out for years. Then one day he hears a bush speak. And we're not talking about a President!

- ■ How did such a spectacular display encourage and motivate Moses?
- ■ Do you think it was plain to Moses that God was speaking? Explain.

Bushes don't usually break out into flames, much less speak about holy ground. But that day Moses heard the voice of God. Amazing! God may not provide you or me with fireworks when he speaks. But we need to get to know him through his Word so that we recognize his voice and understand his message—no matter how he chooses to talk to us. Let's make a sparkling bush in a bottle to remind us of how God spoke to Moses.

- ■ Name things that make it hard for you to listen to God, things that cause "static" and "interference" and distract you from his voice.

Distribute the bottled water, one per child. Have kids open bottles and take turns pouring half the water from their bottles into the pitcher. Push a snip of evergreen branch or a leaf cutting into each bottle. Use a funnel to fill the rest of the bottle with corn syrup.

- ■ Why do you think God spoke to Moses in such an unusual way?
- ■ What made that place "holy ground"?

Have kids add about 15 pieces of confetti to the bottles.

Now repeat today's Bible verse while vigorously shaking your bottles. As the corn syrup diffuses, the water will become clear.

> "Show me your ways, O Lord, teach me your paths" Psalm 25:4.

Observe what happens! (*The flecks of red and orange "flames" (confetti) stay suspended in and around the evergreen "bush."*)

God's messages come to us through the Bible and parents and teachers. Other times God speaks quietly to us as we pray. Let's let our sparkling bottle bush remind us that God speaks in many ways—we just need to listen!

Option: Open the bottle of light cooking syrup and drain a little into a cup. Drop a few orange and red sparkle pony beads followed by a sprig of artificial greenery directly into the bottle. Close the cap and shake. In a pinch, can use a bottle of clear, carbonated beverage in place of the corn syrup and a sprig of rosemary sprigs for the pine branch. Dispose of after use.

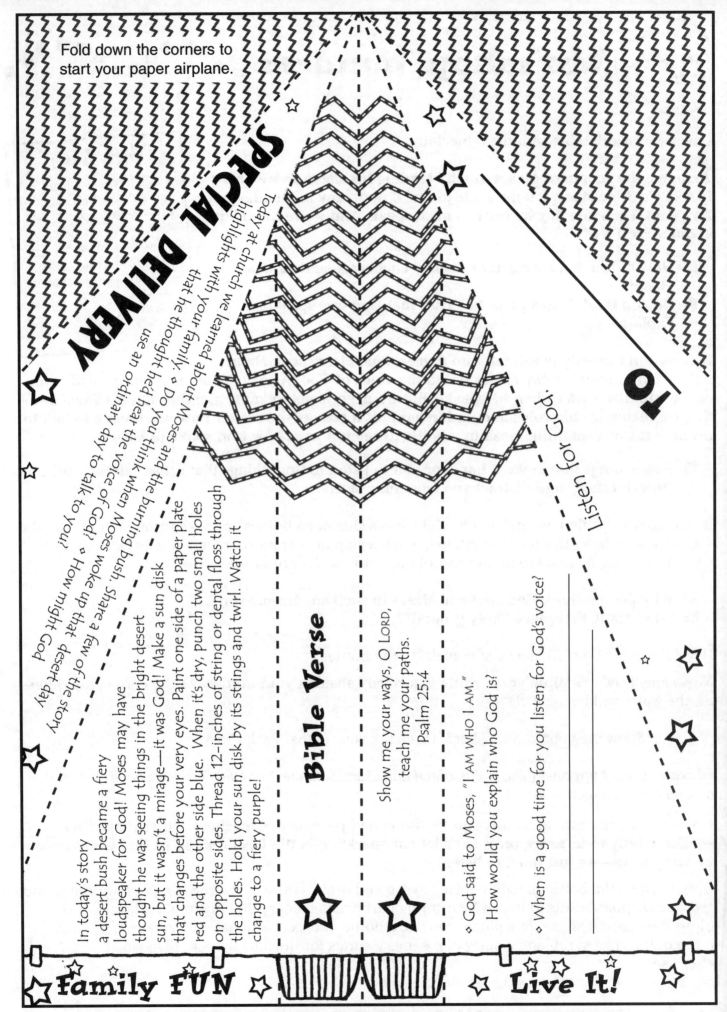

Fold down the corners to start your paper airplane.

SPECIAL DELIVERY

TO

Listen for God.

Today at church we learned about Moses and the burning bush. Share a few of the story highlights with your family. Do you think when Moses woke up that desert day that he thought he'd hear the voice of God? How might God use an ordinary day to talk to you?

In today's story a desert bush became a fiery loudspeaker for God! Moses may have thought he was seeing things in the bright desert sun, but it wasn't a mirage—it was God! Make a sun disk that changes before your very eyes. Paint one side of a paper plate red and the other side blue. When it's dry, punch two small holes on opposite sides. Thread 12-inches of string or dental floss through the holes. Hold your sun disk by its strings and twirl. Watch it change to a fiery purple!

Bible Verse

Show me your ways, O LORD, teach me your paths.
Psalm 25:4

◊ God said to Moses, "I AM WHO I AM."
How would you explain who God is?

◊ When is a good time for you listen for God's voice!

Family FUN

Live It!

Oh, Brother!

Option

Get Set
LARGE GROUP ■ Greet kids and do a puppet skit. Schooner talks about his favorite helper and learns a lesson on helping God's people.

❏ large bird puppet ❏ puppeteer

1

Bible 4U! Instant Drama
LARGE GROUP ■ Moses gives a dramatized account of how he appealed to God for help confronting Pharaoh.

❏ 1 actor ❏ a copy of pp. 30–31, Off to See the Pharaoh script ❏ 4 numbered balls ❏ bag

2

Shepherd's Spot
SMALL GROUP ■ Make paper friends who stand firm when they're connected back-to-back. Autograph each other's handouts in a show of support. Share concerns and pray. Send home the Special Delivery handout.

❏ Bibles ❏ pencils ❏ scissors ❏ glue sticks ❏ copies of p. 34, Two Are Better Than One ❏ copies of p. 36, Special Delivery

Option

Workshop Wonders
SMALL GROUP ■ Do a workshop warm up with M&M® candies. Then make a funny putty that reinforces today's Bible truth.

❏ cookie sheets ❏ M&Ms® candies ❏ pencils ❏ Borax® detergent ❏ warm water ❏ white glue ❏ food coloring ❏ small bowls and tablespoons ❏ newspaper ❏ wet wipes for clean up

Bible Basis
God gives Aaron as a helper
Exodus 3:15–16, 18–20, 4:10–16, 7:6–7

Learn It!
God sends the helpers we need.

Live It!
Work with God's people.

Bible Verse
Two are better than one... if one falls down, his friend can help him up.
Ecclesiastes 4:9–10

Quick Takes

Ex 3:15–16, 18–20, 4:10–16, 7:6–7

God also said to Moses, "Say to the Israelites, 'The Lord, the God of your fathers—the God of Abraham, the God of Isaac and the God of Jacob—has sent me to you.' This is my name forever, the name by which I am to be remembered from generation to generation.

16 "Go, assemble the elders of Israel and say to them, 'The Lord, the God of your fathers—the God of Abraham, Isaac and Jacob—appeared to me and said: I have watched over you and have seen what has been done to you in Egypt.

18 "The elders of Israel will listen to you. Then you and the elders are to go to the king of Egypt and say to him, 'The Lord, the God of the Hebrews, has met with us. Let us take a three-day journey into the desert to offer sacrifices to the Lord our God.'

19 But I know that the king of Egypt will not let you go unless a mighty hand compels him.

20 So I will stretch out my hand and strike the Egyptians with all the wonders that I will perform among them. After that, he will let you go.

4:10 Moses said to the Lord, "O Lord, I have never been eloquent, neither in the past nor since you have spoken to your servant. I am slow of speech and tongue."

11 The Lord said to him, "Who gave man his mouth? Who makes him deaf or mute? Who gives him sight or makes him blind? Is it not I, the Lord?

12 Now go; I will help you speak and will teach you what to say."

13 But Moses said, "O Lord, please send someone else to do it."

14 Then the Lord's anger burned against Moses and he said, "What about your brother, Aaron the Levite? I know he can speak well. He is already on his way to meet you, and his heart will be glad when he sees you.

15 You shall speak to him and put words in his mouth; I will help both of you speak and will teach you what to do.

16 He will speak to the people for you, and it will be as if he were your mouth and as if you were God to him.

7:6 Moses and Aaron did just as the Lord commanded them.

7 Moses was eighty years old and Aaron eighty-three when they spoke to Pharaoh.

Insights

God gave Moses a straightforward and reasonably terrifying job: go to Pharaoh and tell him to let my people go into the desert to worship me.

You've gotta be kidding. I could never do that!

Moses, exiled prince of Egypt, was also the prince of excuses: Moses was a wanted man in Egypt. He'd killed a man, and he wasn't good at public speaking.

On the other hand, God gave Moses compelling reasons to obey.

1. His people had suffered without hope for four hundred years.

2. God gave him miraculous signs to perform and promised to be with him.

3. No one knew the workings of Pharaoh's court better than the adopted prince who'd been raised there did. Though God's anger burned at Moses' reluctance, he ultimately gave Moses a helper—his brother Aaron. Aaron was a good speaker, Moses would tell him what to say, and Aaron would pass on the message to Pharaoh.

God understands human weakness. He could see Moses' quaking heart, and in compassion gave him a human helper who would stand at his side. Kids need to see from this story that God understands our fears and weaknesses. Psalm 103:13-14 reminds us, "As a father has compassion on his children, so the Lord has compassion on those who fear him; for he knows how we are formed, he remembers that we are dust."

Use this lesson to help kids understand that God doesn't give us a huge responsibility, then leave us on our own. He is with us every step of the way. he gives us human helpers to stand at our side and encourage us.

Get Set

Hello! Today is "Two are better than one" day. But don't go home and look for it on your calendar—I just made it up! God sends us helpers so we never have to go it alone. Speaking of which... where's Schooner? *Schooner pops up.*

Schooner: *Squawk!*

Leader: Oh, hello Schooner.

Schooner: Howdy.

Leader: You look very handsome today.

Schooner: Thank you.

Leader: You know, Schooner, I'm glad that you're my helper.

Schooner: Happy to do it, boss.

Leader: Who helps you when you need a hand?

Schooner: You do.

Leader: Thank you. Anyone else?

Schooner: Trixie.

Leader: Trixie?

Schooner: Trixie…my puppy.

Leader: I didn't know you had a dog, Schooner.

Schooner: I do. I love pets.

Leader: Hmm. Some people would say that parrots make good pets.

Schooner: Parrots as pets? Preposterous!

Leader: *(shakes head)* I think so too.

Schooner: Parrots are much too smart and independent to go for a walk or play fetch!

Leader: I agree, Schooner.

Schooner: Parrots need to lead—and not on a leash!

Leader: I agree. I agree!

Schooner: Parrots rule. Pets drool.

Leader: *(shakes head)* I'm sorry I started this.

Schooner: I think I've made my point, boss.

Leader: Let's get back to Trixie.

Schooner: Ah. Trixie.

Leader: So how does Trixie help you?

Schooner: Let's see. Trixie gets the Parrot Times from the driveway each morning. And she fetches my slippers at night.

Leader: Slippers?

Schooner: Slippers.

Leader: I didn't know parrots wore slippers.

Schooner: Each year Auntie Polly makes me a new pair for my birthday. She uses old banana skins and dried peanut shells.

Leader: *(whispers to the group)* Sounds yummy!

Schooner: Comfy? Yes, they're nice and comfy.

Leader: Well, in today's Bible story God sends a helper to help Moses.

Schooner: Is her name Trixie?

Leader: No. His name was Aaron.

Schooner: Funny name for a dog.

Leader: Aaron was Moses' brother.

Schooner: *(shyly)* Oops. Sorry.

Leader: Moses didn't feel up to the task of speaking and leading God's people.

Schooner: Understandable, boss.

Leader: Yes, it's hard to speak in front of people, especially a biggee like an Egyptian Pharaoh.

Schooner: Or in front of a group of kids.

Leader: Yes, that's hard too.

Schooner: Or parrots.

Leader: Can't say I've ever done that, Schooner.

Schooner: They're a tough crowd. *Squawk!*

Leader: I would think so.

Schooner: So Aaron was Moses' helper?

Leader: Yes. God asked Aaron to speak to the Pharaoh to let his people, the Israelites, leave Egypt.

Schooner: And what about Moses?

Leader: Moses would have his work cut out for him too. We'll hear all about it in the lesson today and in the weeks to come.

Schooner: …so sometimes we need helpers to do God's work.

Leader: Excellent deduction, Schooner.

Schooner: With help, we can do the tasks he asks!

Leader: God sends us the helpers we need. Let's I'm ready to hear all about it in Bible 4U! up next.

1 Bible 4U!

No way!

Is this how you'd feel if the local TV station came to your home and asked you to make a speech to the country? Tonight! Would you be nervous? Would you fret and worry? Raise your hand if you would be thinking, *No way, I can't do this. Find someone—anyone—else, please!* Pause as kids respond.

Now what if the TV station told you you could bring a brother or sister or friend to help you? Would you change your mind? Bible 4U! coming on through! Our Bible story today finds the great prophet Moses in such a pickle. God pays him a visit and asks him to do something so hard that Moses tells God no thanks!

As we'll hear, God didn't take Moses response too kindly, but he knew that Moses, with a little help from his brother, Aaron, was the best man to stand before his step-grandfather, the Pharaoh and command the release of his people. Lend me your ears, ladies and gentlemen, and let's hear from the prophet Moses.

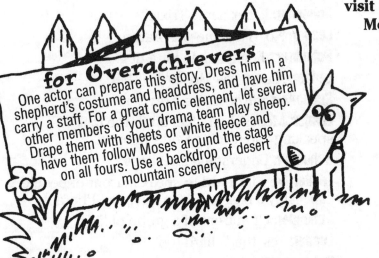

Off to See the Pharaoh
Based on Exodus 3–7

Moses paces back and forth, scratching his head and mumbling to himself.

Okay, so I'm leading my sheep through the desert and all of a sudden this bush bursts into flame and calls my name. You heard me right—a bush called my name! Well, not the bush actually. It was God speaking from the bush. It sounds fantastic, but it's true.

After all these years I've spent as a shepherd, I wondered if God still remembered me. I've been living my life under the radar—out of the spotlight, like an ordinary Joe. I mean, being a former prince of Egypt, I had fame, wealth, and all the finest things the palace could offer. But how could I enjoy all that when my people were suffering in slavery? One day I saw an Egyptian beat one of my people. I killed him. Yes, I killed a man. I had to run away. Far away. So for the last forty years I've been here in Midian. I have a great wife and two sons. It's a quiet life. A good life.

Until this morning, that is. God is sending me back to Egypt to talk Pharaoh into letting my people go free. Oh, man. The thought of facing Pharaoh again makes my stomach turn over. Can you just see it? "Hi, remember me? I'm the adopted kid who grew up here. I use to play by your feet? Anyway, the one true God has had it with the way you're treating his people. Now free them from slavery. Let God's people go!"

That will go over really big, huh? This scares me. This really scares me.

Moses starts pacing again.

And not just the message from God. It's delivering the message that's tough. You know how there are some people who don't mind getting up in front of people and talking? They're smooth, cool and comfortable and they get right to the point. That would not be me. I'm a terrible speaker. I get nervous, my hands sweat, I get butterflies in my stomach and I get my *merds wixed* up. I mean my words mixed up. See what I mean?

I tried to talk God out of sending me. There's go to be somebody who could do a better job. But God made it clear that this was my job and nobody else's. I pleaded with God. I could tell he was getting angry with me. Scary thought, huh?

Finally God promised me a helper—none other than my good ole brother Aaron. Now when Aaron gets in front of an audience, he's smooth. He was born to be a speaker. Looks people right in the eye, never gets nervous or stumbles over his words. Aaron and I will make a dynamic duo. Batman and Robin. Spaghetti and meatballs. Aaron and Moses. Oh, yeah. Doing this with my brother feels a lot better than doing it on my own.

Of course, it's not the two of us who really count. God promised to be with me and tell me what to say. So I get the word from God, pass it on to Aaron, and he makes things perfectly clear to Pharaoh. It sounds like a system. We can do that.

God gave me a tough job. A way tough job. And he knew how scared I was, so he didn't leave me on my own. God is in heaven directing things and Aaron will be at my side getting the word out. Before God gave me a helper, the job seemed impossible. It's still not exactly a walk in the park, but you can't imagine how much better it feels to have someone standing beside me—someone I know I can count on.

God is like that. He may ask you do something hard, but he doesn't leave you out on a limb by yourself. He promises to be with you, and he sends you the helpers you need. It might be your brother or sister, your mom or dad or a friend. It could even be that you're the helper someone else needs!

Well, I'm off to see the Pharaoh. I wonder if he'll recognize me. This is gonna be some adventure. I'll let you all in on it when I get back.

Moses once again looks worried as he walks off stage.

That's if I get back!

Boy, I know just how Moses feels. When you have a hard job in front of you, it's no fun to go it alone. So when I toss out these questions, feel free to get some help from other kids.

Toss the four numbered balls to different parts of the room. Bring the kids with the balls to the front one-by-one and ask these questions. Allow kids to get help from the group if they need it. After each correct answer, let kids drop the ball into a bag.

 ■ **What was the hard job God gave Moses?**

 ■ **Why did God agree to give Moses a helper?**

 ■ **Why was Aaron the perfect guy to be Moses' helper?**

 ■ **When have you done something so hard that you needed a helper to stand beside you and encourage you?**

God knew all about Moses. Remember how God guided that little basket boat down the river to safety? God knew that talking to people made Moses scared and uncomfortable. Because God is loving and kind, he gave Moses just the right person to help him get the job done.

God knows all about you too. He knows if you feel scared before a math test. He knows if your palms get all sweaty in a spelling bee. He knows if meeting new people or reading out loud is really hard for you. Here's the great thing about God: he never leaves you to do hard things on your own. If you need a helper, God will provide one, just as he did for Moses. The God who knows you inside and out won't leave you high and dry in the desert.

Bible Verse
Two are better than one...if one falls down, his friend can help him up.
Ecclesiastes 4:9–10

There's nothing more wonderful than working with God's people. You'll find out more about that in your shepherd groups today.

Dismiss kids to their shepherd groups.

2 Shepherd's Spot

Gather kids in your small group and help them find Exodus 3 in their Bibles. If you have sticky notes on hand, help kids mark the following passages: Exodus 3:15-16, 18-20, 4:10-16, 7:6-7. Ask volunteers to read the passages aloud.

■ **God gave Moses a tough job. What kind of hard job do you think God might ask you to do someday?** Pause as kids respond.

Moses was one of the greatest leaders God ever sent to his people. But even great men need help. Together Moses and Aaron faced down mean old Pharaoh and delivered God's message.

Do you know who God has given you for helpers? Look around! The people in this room—in this church—are ready to give you the kind of help Aaron gave Moses. Together, with God's guidance, we can do much more than any one of us could do alone. Today's handout will show you just what I mean.

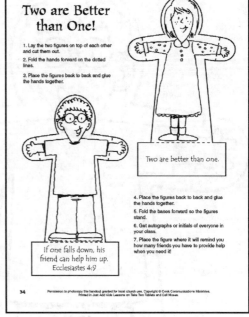

Distribute copies of Two are Better than One handout. Have kids cut out the two figures. **Try standing one of these guys on his own. Pretty wobbly, isn't he? But when we put them together, they pull it together and become strong.** Ask a volunteer to read the Bible Verse on the base, then encourage kids to sign each other's figures. Show them how to stand the figures back to back and glue their hands together.

When you look at these guys, you'll see the autographs of all the people in this class who are ready to be your encouragers and helpers. How cool is that!

Praying for people is one of the best ways to help. You can be my encouragers today by praying for something I've been concerned about. Mention a prayer concern and encourage kids to do the same. Then close with prayer. **Dear Lord, we see how you understood Moses. Thank you for understanding us in the same way. Thank you for giving us friends who encourage us in the jobs we have to do for you. Right now we pray for** (mention each child's requests). **Help us to look for helpers from you when we need them. And remind us when others need our help. In Jesus' name, amen.**

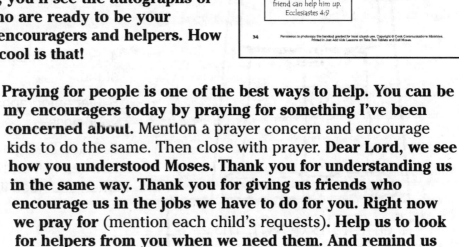

Two are Better than One!

1. Lay the two figures on top of each other and cut them out.

2. Fold the hands forward on the dotted lines.

3. Place the figures back to back and glue the hands together.

Two are better than one.

If one falls down, his friend can help him up. Ecclesiastes 4:9

4. Fold the bases forward so the figures stand.

5. Get autographs or initials of everyone in your class.

5. Place the figure where it will remind you how many friends you have to provide help when you need it!

You'll need one cookie sheet for every five to six students.

Get List:
- ☐ M&Ms® candies
- ☐ cookie sheets
- ☐ pencils
- ☐ Borax® detergent
- ☐ warm water
- ☐ white glue
- ☐ food coloring
- ☐ small bowls and tablespoons
- ☐ newspaper
- ☐ wet wipes for clean up

To start our workshop time let's do a little warm-up exercise. Pour the hard-shelled candies onto the cookie sheet. Hand each student a pencil. **We often need help to accomplish what God wants us to do. God knows that it can be hard to go it alone.** Pick up a pencil. **For our warm up, see how many candies you can get into your mouth by using only the tool I gave you—a pencil. Be sure to place your free hand behind your back and keep your head up. Ready? Go it alone!** Your kids are apt to try several ingenious methods to get the candy into their mouths. After a bit, say, **Let's make this process a bit easier by helping one other.** Ask kids to work with a neighbor to take turns picking up the candies using both pencil erasers and then dropping the candies into their mouths. **A little help goes a long way. Great job!**

Put candies and trays aside. **It's funny putty time! As we measure and combine the ingredients let's remember that each ingredient by itself is just that…one simple ingredient. But when we combine ingredients we form a binding polymer. In other words, a strong compound that can do much!**

Combine the Borax powder with 1/2 cup of warm water. Kids can take turns stirring until the Borax dissolves. The mixture should "feel" gritty.

■ **What five fun things can you come up with that might help the nursery workers in our church?**

In another bowl have another group of kids mix 5 ounces of white glue and 8 drops of food coloring until blended.

■ **Share a favorite "helping others" story that you're not likely to forget.**

Stir the Borax mixture into the glue mixture bit by bit. The mixture will thicken. Knead the mixture. *It is very sticky!* Keep kneading until you create a stretchy, pliable putty. **When the polymer molecules join each other they become very strong. This helps us see that when we work together for the Lord, we become strong enough to get the job done.**

Separate your class into four groups. Cut the putty in four pieces and distribute along with the newspaper. **Take turns gently stretching your funny putty. Now see if you can find one word from today's Bible Verse in this newspaper. The larger the word the better!** Today's verse:

Two are better than one, if one falls down, his friend can help him up. Ecclesiastes 4:9

Good! Now press your funny putty onto the word. Press hard. Then lift the putty. Take a look. The Bible Verse word will appear on the putty—albeit backwards! **I guess that's why they call it *funny putty!*** Have kids take turns finding words and kneading the putty after each use. Hand out the wet wipes to clean newsprint from fingers and hands.

Fold down the corners to start your paper airplane.

SPECIAL DELIVERY

TO

Work with God's people.

Family FUN

Make a nifty sign to hang on a bedroom doorknob to let others know you're available to help. Grab a coffee can lid, pen, paper clip and box of crayons. Use the pen to write "Helper In!" along with your name on the lid. Now open the paper clip and scratch deep designs into the plastic. Circles, loops, wavy lines will look good. Color in each design. Use a tissue to polish away any extra crayon from the plastic. Punch two holes in the top of your sign and make a ribbon hanger. Slip over a doorknob and be "on call," ready to help!

Today at church we learned how God told Moses to do both encouraging and scary. Why was what God gave Moses to do both encouraging and scary? Share a time when a friend helped your family accomplish a hard job.

Bible Verse

Two are better than one...if one falls down, his friend can help him up.
Ecclesiastes 4:9–10

Live It!

◊ Can you think of someone you know who really needs a helper?

◊ What's the most fun you ever had working together with God's people?

Ribbit, Buzz, Crunch—EEK!

Option

Get Set
LARGE GROUP ■ Greet kids and do a puppet skit. Schooner learns of God's power and Pharaoh's broken promises.

❑ large bird puppet ❑ puppeteer

1

Bible 4U! Instant Drama
LARGE GROUP ■ An Egyptian brother and sister tell of their experiences during the plagues of Egypt.

❑ 2 actors ❑ copies of pp. 40–41, A Tale of Two Egyptians script ❑ 4 numbered balls ❑ bag ❑ chewing gum

2

Shepherd's Spot
SMALL GROUP ■ Create a card with a frog that reminds us to "Be Cool, God Rules". Share concerns and pray. Send home the Special Delivery handout.

❑ Bibles ❑ pencils ❑ scissors ❑ glue sticks ❑ copies of p. 44, Be Cool
❑ copies of p. 46, Special Delivery

Option

Workshop Wonders
SMALL GROUP ■ Have some marble-ous fun! Hit the mark (Pharaoh's heart) with the power of God's Word.

❑ Bibles ❑ bottled water ❑ red food coloring ❑ frog toy ❑ bug spray
❑ fly swatter ❑ stuffed animal ❑ box of bandages ❑ ice cube tray
❑ apple ❑ flashlight ❑ doll ❑ scissors ❑ paper plate ❑ marble

Bible Basis
The plagues of Egypt.
Exodus 5:1–2;
7:1–11:1

Learn It!
God's power can save us.

Live It!
Believe in God's power.

Bible Verse
Be strong in the Lord and in his mighty power.
Ephesians 6:10

Quick Takes

Afterwards Moses and Aaron went to Pharaoh and said, "This is what the Lord, the God of Israel, says: 'Let my people go, so that they may hold a festival to me in the desert.'"

2 Pharaoh said, "Who is the Lord, that I should obey him and let Israel go? I do not know the Lord and I will not let Israel go."

Excerpts from chapters 7–11

7:20 Moses and Aaron did just as the Lord had commanded. He raised his staff in the presence of Pharaoh and his officials and struck the water of the Nile, and all the water was changed into blood. 21 The fish in the Nile died, and the river smelled so bad that the Egyptians could not drink its water. Blood was everywhere in Egypt.

8:5 Then the Lord said to Moses, "Tell Aaron, 'Stretch out your hand with your staff over the streams and canals and ponds, and make frogs come up on the land of Egypt.'" 6 Aaron stretched out his hand over the waters of Egypt, and the frogs came up and covered the land. 17 When Aaron stretched out his hand with the staff and struck the dust of the ground, gnats came upon men and animals. All the dust throughout the land of Egypt became gnats. 24 …Dense swarms of flies poured into Pharaoh's palace and into the houses of his officials, and throughout Egypt the land was ruined by the flies.

9:6 …All the livestock of the Egyptians died, but not one animal belonging to the Israelites died. 10 So they took soot from a furnace and stood before Pharaoh. Moses tossed it into the air, and festering boils broke out on men and animals. 25 Throughout Egypt hail struck everything in the fields—both men and animals; it beat down everything growing in the fields and stripped every tree.

10:13 So Moses stretched out his staff over Egypt, and the Lord made an east wind blow across the land all that day and all that night. By morning the wind had brought the locusts. 14 they invaded all Egypt and settled down in every area of the country in great numbers. Never before had there been such a plague of locusts, nor will there ever be again. 22 So Moses stretched out his hand towards the sky, and total darkness covered all Egypt for three days.

11:1 Now the Lord said to Moses, "I will bring one more plague on Pharaoh and on Egypt. After that, he will let you go from here, and when he does, he will drive you out completely.

Insights

Piles of reeking frogs!

A line from a comic book? No—an all too real predicament for the Egyptians. When Moses told Pharaoh to let God's people go; a contest of wills began. Pharaoh, the absolute ruler of the mightiest kingdom on earth, wasn't about to take orders from Moses, even if Moses did come as a representative of the living God.

And so the plagues began, ten of them in all: water to blood, frogs, gnats, flies, dying livestock, boils, hail, locusts, darkness and death of the firstborn. At first, Pharaoh told Moses to get lost. When the frogs invaded, Pharaoh promised to let the people go if Moses prayed for the frogs to go away. Of course, as soon as the frogs were gone, Pharaoh went back on his word. And so it went.

When God sent flies to cover Egypt, he kept his people in Goshen safe from the pestilence. When the Egyptian livestock died, Hebrew livestock remained healthy. And so on.

So what was the point of all the plagues? God explained it to Pharaoh: "By now I could have stretched out my hand and struck you and your people with a plague that would have wiped you off the earth. But I have raised you up for this very purpose, that I might show you my power and that my name might be proclaimed in all the earth" (Ex. 9:15–16).

Pharaoh thought nothing of the suffering of hundreds of thousands of slaves. He didn't hesitate to lie to God and man.

What consolation can kids take from this story? Evil men will have their day, but God is not oblivious to the suffering of his people. He provides for them and protects them, and when the time is right he will make a way out. And in the process, he'll make his name great among all the nations of the world. This message is every bit as much for our time as was in ancient times.

Option Get Set

Welcome! Today's Bible story is a real zapper. I hope you're ready for it. You'll hear how God used his power to help his people—not once or twice, but many times. God wanted the selfish Pharaoh to let his people go free. Schooner, join me and we'll share what we know with the group. *Schooner pops up.*

Leader: Hello, my friend.

Schooner: *Squawk!* Top of the morning to you!

Leader: I'd like to talk today about promises.

Schooner: Goodie. Goodie.

Leader: A promise is a gift.

Schooner: Something with a bright green bow?

Leader: Not exactly, but it's a gift nonetheless.

Schooner: Explain, please.

Leader: Let's see. A promise is a gift that someone with a good heart wants to give to someone else.

Schooner: But a gift comes in a box, boss.

Leader: Well…sometimes.

Schooner: And it's something you can see…or wear…or play with.

Leader: Oh, Schooner, some of the best gifts can't be seen or touched.

Schooner: What do you mean?

Leader: God's power is a gift.

Schooner: I never thought about that.

Leader: And God's promises.

Schooner: Hmm. Two gifts!

Leader: Plus, there's a bonus. God's promises are weatherproof!

Schooner: Huh?

Leader: You can count on them to shine—always. Through rain or hail or flying bugs.

Schooner: I…get it, I think.

Leader: Our powerful God delivers his promises without fail to those he loves.

Schooner: *I* believe in God's power.

Leader: Good for you, my friend!

Schooner: *Squawk!*

Leader: In today's Bible story, a wicked Pharaoh makes a promise to the Old Testament brothers Aaron and Moses.

Schooner: A promise…a gift without a box or bow!

Leader: Not this time, Schooner.

Schooner: No gift?

Leader: That's right. In today's story, Pharaoh promises Aaron and Moses that he will let God's people leave Egypt.

Schooner: Sounds like a plan.

Leader: And it was…God's plan.

Schooner: So what happens?

Leader: Pharaoh, the great pretender, breaks his promise.

Schooner: But…but he said he would!

Leader: More than once, Schooner.

Schooner: This is how I see, it, boss. Pharaoh's promise was not a gift.

Leader: Imagine making promises knowing you'll break 'em!

Schooner: I've learned something, boss.

Leader: Yes?

Schooner: Pharaoh's promises are not weatherproof!

Leader: *(shakes head)* As we'll hear very soon in today's Bible story.

Schooner: Broken promises. That must have made God angry.

Leader: God, the Great Promisekeeper, used his power to let Pharaoh know that he is Lord.

Schooner: When I make a promise I try to keep it.

Leader: Good job, Schooner. Too bad Pharaoh didn't make a promise to keep his promises.

Schooner: Did God's people ever get to leave?

Leader: Well, that would be giving away the story.

Schooner: An impatient bird can only take so much!

Leader: Bible 4U! up next!

1 Bible 4U!

Hey, it's time for another live action presentation of Bible 4U! Today we're traveling to the country of Egypt where some highly unusual events are about to occur. First there's one disaster, then another and another, and another and…you get the point. What's with all the disasters, you ask? Well, it's a case of almighty God against a powerful king with a hard, cruel heart.

God's people have been slaves in Egypt for hundreds of years. God has sent Moses and Aaron to say, "Enough already! God says to let his people go." Pharaoh isn't used to having anyone tell him what to do. He isn't about to obey. He likes having all those slaves to do his work. But God has prepared Moses and Aaron to do mighty miracles that will save and protect his people. You can't even imagine what's about to happen to the people of Egypt—all because their king won't obey God. Let's drop in on one Egyptian family and see how a brother and sister deal with disaster.

Instant Prep
Before class, ask for two volunteers to play an Egyptian brother and sister. Give them copies of the script below, "A Tale of Two Egyptians" and a piece of chewing gum.

for Overachievers
Have a drama team prepare the story. Dress the Egyptian brother and sister in white tunics with shiny gold belts and collars. Dress other drama team members in black. At the appropriate moments, have them enter and play the frogs, gnats and flies. Use a backdrop ground or set that represents a simple Egyptian home.

A Tale of Two Egyptians
Based on Exodus 5:1–2; 7:1–11:1

Two Egyptian children sit near their home. They're bored. They "snap" their gum and draw circles in the dirt with their fingers.

Boy: Mom said to go to the river and get water. You want to come with me?

Girl: *(sighs and snaps gum)* Why not? I'm bored anyway. It's not like they've invented Barbie dolls yet.

They walk, as if going to the river.

Boy: *(makes a face)* Do you smell something really yucky?

Girl: Yeah. I wonder…*(looks down)* Oh my goodness, look at the river. That's not water, it's, it's…

Boy: Blood! The river has turned to blood.

Both cover their faces with their hands and yell, then run away. After a moment, they cautiously return.

Girl: *(still out of breath)* I heard that men named Moses and Aaron did that blood thing to the river.

Boy: Sure! I remember now. They wanted Pharaoh to let all the Hebrew slaves go free. Like that's gonna happen!

Girl: Um, did your pet frog get out of its cage?

Boy: I don't have a pet frog.

Girl: Then why is there a frog hopping around the room? Oh, my goodness!

Boy: One…two. three…they're everywhere! They're everywhere!

Girl: Frogs in the oven, frogs in the bed, frogs in the soup, frogs in the bread!

Both cover their faces with their hands and yell, then run away. After a moment, they cautiously return.

Boy: That was intense. I always sorta' liked frogs until this happened. I don't ever want to see another frog in my whole life.

Girl: Did that Moses guy do this too?

Boy: Yep. He still wants Pharaoh to let the Hebrew slaves go free.

Girl: Do you think we'll have more disasters like this?

Boy: I can't say for sure, but I wouldn't be surprised. The God of the Hebrews isn't like the idols we worship. He isn't made of stone. He doesn't just sit there. He does things for his people.

Girl: Maybe Pharaoh should let the slaves go. We don't need any more of this.

Boy: Don't look now, but there's a huge swarm of gnats coming this way. Duck!

Girl: Oh my goodness, gnats and ducks?!

They drop to the floor and cover their heads with their hands. After a moment, they look up.

Girl: Is it safe?

Boy: Maybe.

They get up, brush themselves off and look around.

Girl: Do you hear what I hear?

Boy: Flies!

Girl: Millions and billions of flies!

Boy: Hide!

Girl: Not again!

They scurry around, then come back to the center, drop to the floor and cover their heads with their hands.

Boy: *(peeks out)* The buzzing is gone. *(stands)* All clear!

Girl: *(still hiding)* Are you sure?

Boy: Get up already!

Girl: *(stands and shakes herself)* Okay, which was worse—the gnats or the flies?

Boy: Neither one was as bad as all the cattle and sheep dying. *(Scratches head)* Hmm. Did you notice that not a single animal that belongs to the slaves died?

Girl: *(looks to the horizon)* And when that terrible hailstorm pounded all the crops and stripped the trees here in Egypt, the land of Goshen where the slaves live didn't get one single hail stone?

Boy: Do you get the feeling that we're serving the wrong God?

Girl: I do, I really do. I mean, while all these disasters have happened to us, the God of the Hebrews has protected them.

Boy: I think their God is gonna win.

Girl: What do you mean?

Boy: I think terrible things are going to keep happening until Pharaoh lets the slaves go.

Girl: Pharaoh never gives in to anybody. And he wants those slaves to keep building his cities.

Boy: Well, this time Pharaoh has met his match. Unless he lets God's people go free, I fear all of Egypt will be destroyed.

Girl: Where would they go? Into the desert?

Boy: Sure. If God protected them from all the things that happened here, he could take care of them in the desert.

Girl: I wish I knew more about their God.

Boy: I wish I knew what the next disaster was going to be.

Girl: Lemme' see, have we done locusts yet?

Boy: *(rolls eyes)* Bad idea. Really bad idea.

Girl: Do you hear that sound?

Boy: What sound? *(listens)* Do you mean that snap, crackle and crunch sound?

Girl: Locusts. Oh my goodness!

Boy: On your mark, get set…run!

They both run off stage yelling.

Bible 4U!

Disaster city, huh? That was pretty bad, if you were an Egyptian. If you were one of God's people, you learned what it means to be under God's protection. Ready for the great ball toss? Grab one if it comes your way.

Toss the four numbered balls to different parts of the room. Bring the kids with the balls to the front one-by-one and ask these questions. Allow kids to get help from the group if they need it. After each correct answer, let kids drop the ball into a bag.

 ■ **Why did all these terrible things happen to the Egyptian people?**

 ■ **Why didn't these disaster happen to the Hebrew slaves?**

 ■ **Why wouldn't Pharaoh obey God and let the slaves go free?**

 ■ **If you were one of the kids in today's story and you got a chance to talk to Pharaoh, what would you say?**

Bible Verse
Be strong in the Lord and in his mighty power.
Ephesians 6:10

You know, I think those Egyptian kids in our story were pretty smart. If I were in their shoes, I'd want to be on God's side too! Can you imagine what it must have been like to have all these terrible things happen to you while God kept his people safe?

I might go stand by the palace and yell, "Hey, Pharaoh. Get a clue. You're gonna' lose. You may be the greatest king on earth, but you're nothing compared to the God of the Hebrews. Just look at them. They're safe and sound. And look at us. We've had gnats and flies and locusts and hail and sores on our bodies and all kinds of terrible stuff. Give it up, Pharaoh. Obey God and let his people go." Of course anyone who actually said that wouldn't live very long.

But if I were a Hebrew slave, I'd be thinking, "Wow! Isn't God amazing? Have you seen all the stuff he's done to the Egyptians to get Pharaoh to let us go? Boy, am I glad to be on God's side. I believe God really is going to get us out of here."

Being on God's side is the best place you can ever be. When bad stuff happens, you know he can take care of you. Today in your shepherd groups you'll learn more about believing in God's power.

Dismiss kids to their shepherd groups.

42

2 Shepherd's Spot.

Help kids find Exodus 5 and 7 in their Bibles. Pick verses that highlight today's story and ask volunteers to read the passages aloud.

When Pharaoh wouldn't let God's people go, God sent 10 terrible disasters on Egypt. We call them the ten plagues. You'll find them all listed here on this card. Distribute the "Be Cool" handouts (p. 44). Check them out.

■ **If you had to pick one plague to live through, which one would you choose?**

Fortunately, God's people didn't have to make that choice. God kept them safe through everything that happened. We can learn all kinds of lessons from this story.

■ **What important things does this story teach you?** (*God is more powerful than anyone is; God takes care of his people; even when terrible things happen, God is in control.*)

See the frog on the card? He's telling you to be cool because God rules! There's a verse from the book of Ephesians that's a really great one to remember. Have kids read the verse aloud together. **If you believe that God can help you be strong, sign your name on the line above the verse. Then turn to the person on your left and say: (name), be strong in the Lord and in his mighty power.**

Have kids cut out the cards and fold both ends toward the center with the frog on top.

■ **Do you see any terrible things like the plagues happening in our world today?**

Use your cool froggie as a reminder that God rules!

Invite kids to share their concerns, then close with prayer. **Heavenly Father, you are great. Greater than we can imagine. So great that we can trust you even when terrible things happen. We pray for** (mention each child's request). **Thank you for your great power. Help us to trust you and stand strong. In Jesus' name, amen.**

Be Cool!

Check out our frog friend on the card. He's cool. Know why? Because in the midst of all the terrible things that happened in Egypt, God rules! And that's important for you to know. Nothing is a surprise to God. He rules, no matter what!

1. Cut out the card.

2. If you believe God rules, sign your name on the line above the Bible verse. That's your reminder that the mightiest power belongs to God, so you can be strong!

3. Fold the section you just signed toward the center. Then fold the frog to the center so it makes the cover of the card.

Be strong in the Lord and in his mighty power.
Ephesians 6:10

Be cool. God rules!

hail
darkness
locusts
sick animals
gnats
frogs
water to blood
firstborn dies
boils
flies

"Option" Workshop Wonders

The items in today's *Get List* represent each of the plagues that Egypt suffered in the Bible story. Before class "bloody" the bottled water with the red food coloring. Then drop the bottled water as well as the other listed items into a shopping bag. Finally, cut a heart from the center of a paper plate. Set the heart aside and place the paper plate upside down on the floor. Have kids grab their Bibles and sit in a circle around the plate. Join them with a marble and the shopping bag.

God is powerful. The Egyptians and Israelites saw a glimpse of his power first hand. But Pharaoh wasn't buying it. With every plague, Pharaoh remained stubbornly unimpressed with God's power. No matter how long his people suffered, Pharaoh's heart remained "heartless"—cold to Aaron and Moses' plea to let the Israelites leave Egypt. Hold up the paper plate with the heart cut-out.

- ■ Have you ever been in a situation that looked hopeless? Do you believe in your heart of hearts that God can save you?
- ■ What part of today's powerful story can you share with someone who doesn't know anything about God?

Let's take turns shooting God's power into Pharaoh's stubborn heart! Hold up the marble. **Flick your finger to send the marble rolling. Once your marble drops into the heart cutout reach into my bag and pull out one item. Look it over. Then tell us the connection between the item and one of the plagues from today's story. The rest of us will find that passage in the Old Testament book of Exodus in our Bibles.** For your convenience, the plagues and matching items are listed below:

> Blood-*bottled water,* (Exodus 7:14–24;) Frogs-*frog toy,* (Exodus 8:1–15); Gnats-*bug spray,* (Exodus 8:16–19); Flies-*fly swatter,* (Exodus 8:20–32); Livestock-*stuffed animals,* (Exodus 9:1–7); Boils-*bandages,* (Exodus 9:8–12); Hail-*ice cube tray,* (Exodus 9:13–35); Locusts-*apple (Crunch! Munch! Ask a student to take a bite.),* (Exodus 10:1–10); Darkness-*flashlight,* (Exodus 10:21–29).

Hit the mark every time! Let's always remember to believe in God's power. Moses never gave up. He kept going back and demanding that Pharaoh, "Let God's people go!" In the end, God's power made all the difference.

If you choose (and have enough supplies), divide your class into groups and hand a bag or sack off to each. Or make "plague" stations and have kids shoot marbles into paper plate cut-outs to collect small, representative items to add to their individual paper sacks. Don't forget to put Bibles marked with the appropriate Scripture passage at each station.

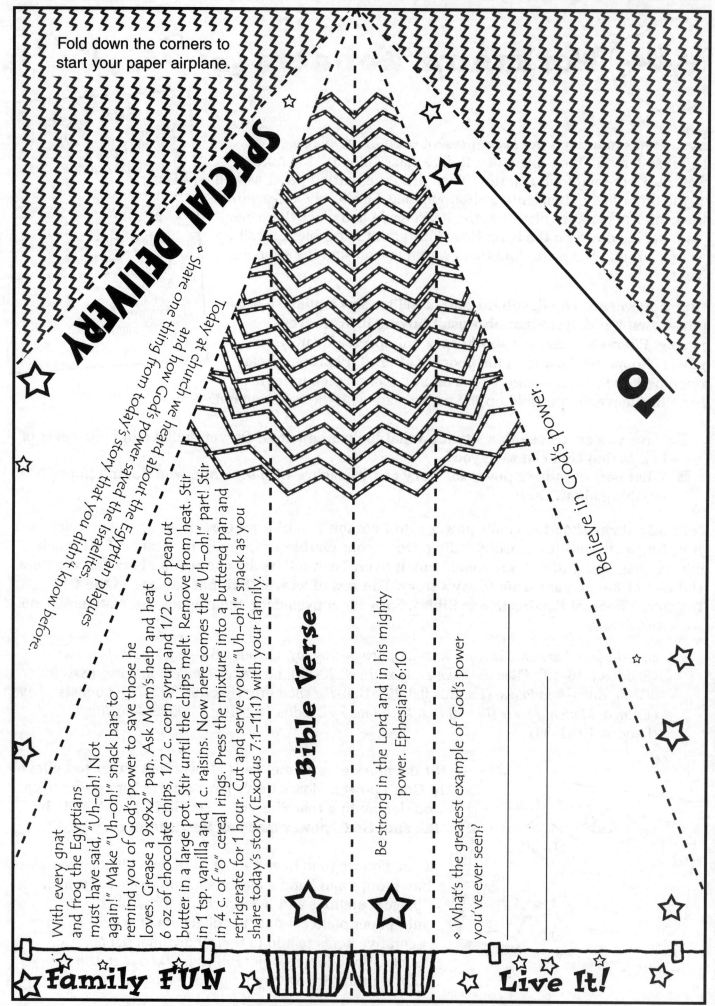

Fold down the corners to start your paper airplane.

SPECIAL DELIVERY

TO

Believe in God's power.

"Share one thing from today's story that you didn't know before."

Today at church we heard about the Egyptian plagues and how God's power saved the Israelites.

With every gnat and frog the Egyptians must have said, "Uh-oh! Not again!" Make "Uh-oh!" snack bars to remind you of God's power to save those he loves. Grease a 9x9x2" pan. Ask Mom's help and heat 6 oz of chocolate chips, 1/2 c. corn syrup and 1/2 c. of peanut butter in a large pot. Stir until the chips melt. Remove from heat. Stir in 1 tsp. vanilla and 1 c. raisins. Now here comes the "Uh-oh!" part! Stir in 4 c. of "o" cereal rings. Press the mixture into a buttered pan and refrigerate for 1 hour. Cut and serve your "Uh-oh!" snack as you share today's story (Exodus 7:1–11:1) with your family.

Bible Verse

Be strong in the Lord and in his mighty power. Ephesians 6:10

◇ What's the greatest example of God's power you've ever seen?

Family FUN

Live It!

Passed Over

Option

Get Set
LARGE GROUP ■ Greet kids and do a puppet skit. Schooner discovers that a picnic lunch is cause for celebration.

❑ large bird puppet ❑ puppeteer

1

Bible 4U! Instant Drama
LARGE GROUP ■ Two teens discuss the preparation of a Passover meal as they get ready for their great escape from Egypt.

❑ 2 actors ❑ copies of pp. 50–51, The Great Escape script ❑ 4 numbered balls
❑ bag Optional: ❑ 2 Bibletime costumes

2

Shepherd's Spot
SMALL GROUP ■ Create a folding booklet that explains how Passover reminds us of Jesus' sacrifice. Share concerns and pray together. Send home the Special Delivery handout.

❑ Bibles ❑ pencils ❑ scissors ❑ copies of p. 54, Invitation to a Feast
❑ copies of p. 56, Special Delivery

Option

Workshop Wonders
SMALL GROUP ■ Choose between two snacks. Or form two groups and make them both to experience the taste of Passover.

(Recipe 1) ❑ plastic knives or chopper ❑ bowl ❑ apples ❑ chopped almonds
❑ sugar ❑ cinnamon ❑ grated lemon rind ❑ grape juice ❑ napkins ❑ serving cups
and spoons (Recipe 2) ❑ matzo crackers ❑ quick hardening chocolate syrup
❑ wax paper ❑ cookie tray ❑ crushed nuts

Bible Basis
Passover
Exodus 12:1–3,
7–8, 12–14,
25–29

Learn It!
God's Word
brings life.

Live It!
Follow God's
Word.

Bible Verse
Now choose life, so that you and your children may live and that you may love the Lord your God, listen to his voice, and hold fast to him.
Deuteronomy 30:19–20

Quick Takes

Exodus 12:1–3, 7–8, 12–14, 25–29

The Lord said to Moses and Aaron in Egypt, 2 "This month is to be for you the first month, the first month of your year. 3 Tell the whole community of Israel that on the tenth day of this month each man is to take a lamb for his family, one for each household.

7 Then they are to take some of the blood and put it on the sides and tops of the doorframes of the houses where they eat the lambs. 8 That same night they are to eat the meat roasted over the fire, along with bitter herbs, and bread made without yeast.

12 "On that same night I will pass through Egypt and strike down every firstborn—both men and animals—and I will bring judgment on all the gods of Egypt. I am the Lord. 13 The blood will be a sign for you on the houses where you are; and when I see the blood, I will pass over you. No destructive plague will touch you when I strike Egypt.

14 "This is a day you are to commemorate; for the generations to come you shall celebrate it as a festival to the Lord—a lasting ordinance. 25 When you enter the land that the Lord will give you as he promised, observe this ceremony. 26 And when your children ask you, `What does this ceremony mean to you?' 27 then tell them, `It is the Passover sacrifice to the Lord, who passed over the houses of the Israelites in Egypt and spared our homes when he struck down the Egyptians.'" Then the people bowed down and worshiped. 28 The Israelites did just what the Lord commanded Moses and Aaron.

29 At midnight the Lord struck down all the firstborn in Egypt, from the firstborn of Pharaoh, who sat on the throne, to the firstborn of the prisoner, who was in the dungeon, and the firstborn of all the livestock as well.

Insights

Passover is a defining moment for the nation of Israel. And its actions and symbols provide an incredible link to defining moments of our faith in Christ. From ancient practices to the modern Jewish Seder (Passover Feast), we Christians are forever linked to the Jews who followed God's instructions.

God's "menu" for this meal begins with a perfect male lamb. He was to be killed, roasted and eaten, and his blood wiped on the sides and tops of the doorframes of each Hebrew home. For Christians, Jesus is our perfect lamb. Peter called him "a lamb without blemish or defect" (1 Peter 1:19). And his blood was spilled on the wooden frame of the cross.

The bitter herbs in the Seder meal represent the bitter years of slavery in Egypt. We Christians knew bitter slavery to sin before Christ set us free. He took all the bitterness of our sin on the cross. "For we know that our old self was crucified with him so that the body of sin might be done away with, that we should no longer be slaves to sin" (Romans 6:6). In the symbolism of Passover, we see the solemn acknowledgement that Christ's sacrifice removes the bitterness of our sin.

And they were to eat unleavened bread. Hurry, there's no time to let the bread rise! As Christians we think of Jesus at the Last Supper. "And he took bread, gave thanks and broke it, and gave it to them, saying, `This is my body given for you; do this in remembrance of me'" (Luke 22:19).

The Hebrews who obeyed lived. We who choose to accept Jesus' sacrifice do well to hold these events in sacred memory. Use this lesson to help kids understand that as the Israelites who obeyed God's commands chose life, they too can choose life by accepting Jesus' sacrifice for their sins.

Option Get Set

Hey—look at all the wonderful people in this room! Are you ready for a feast? Today's story is about the very first Passover Feast. It happened in Egypt long ago. I think Schooner is pretty excited about what we're learning today. *Schooner pops up.*

Schooner: Did somebody mention my name?
Leader: Hello, Schooner.

Schooner: *(fidgety)* I'm a very excited bird.
Leader: We can see that.

Schooner: I've got big plans for the afternoon.
Leader: Something outdoors?

Schooner: Most certainly!
Leader: Something fun?

Schooner: Yes!
Leader: Something edible?

Schooner: Edible?
Leader: Will there be food, Schooner?

Schooner: You betcha!
Leader: Well, tell us all about it, little birdie.

Schooner: *(proudly)* I'm off with a group of friends to celebrate T.F. Day.
Leader: What's that?

Schooner: Top Flyers Day. It celebrates the day my friends and I learned to fly. We hold it on the same day every year.
Leader: Your first big step, so to speak.

Schooner: And whatever the weather—it's a picnic in the park.
Leader: Sounds like a day to remember.

Schooner: *(extra-fidgety)* So I can't be late, boss. Birds are counting on me. Can we speed this along, pleeeeease?
Leader: Hold on to your tail feathers, Schooner.

Schooner: *(twitches)* That puts me in an awkward position, boss.
Leader: It just so happens that today's Bible story has something to do with a celebration.

Schooner: You don't say?
Leader: And food.

Schooner: Really?
Leader: And the great outdoors!

Schooner: This I gotta hear.
Leader: We know how the leaders Aaron and Moses pleaded with Pharaoh to let the Israelites leave Egypt.

Schooner: But he wouldn't let them go, right?
Leader: But in today's Bible story God prepares the Israelites for the trip. They're going!

Schooner: Did they pack a picnic lunch?
Leader: Let's say that food was very important.

Schooner: Of course! It was a special day.
Leader: A day that God wanted them to remember year after year.

Schooner: Like Top Flyers Day!
Leader: God's people would remember the day as the Feast of Passover.

Schooner: They must have gone all out. Nuts, fresh fruit, crackers…
Leader: Crackers come pretty close, Schooner.

Schooner: What about the rest of the meal?
Leader: Think of it as fast food.

Schooner: Oh. Hamburgers and fries. Great picnic food!
Leader: More like lamburgers. And hold the fries.

Schooner: But you said…
Leader: Once the Pharaoh gave the thumbs up, the Israelites had to be ready to move.

Schooner: That fast, huh?
Leader: Not later that week. Not next month. Right then! The food the Israelites made had to be quick to prepare and quick to eat.

Schooner: Hmm. I'm wondering, boss.
Leader: Yes?

Schooner: What made Pharaoh finally change his mind and let God's people go?
Leader: God's judgement and his almighty power. We'll hear more about it in the fun Bible 4U! up next.

Schooner: I'm there!

1 Bible 4U!

It's so good to see you for this week's Bible 4U! theater. It's the time of Moses. In your hands you hold the very last brick you'll ever make as a slave under Egyptian rule. Moses, your leader of hope, has just given you the good news. It's quitting time! Pharaoh has finally—finally! —let you go.

Quickly you wash your muddy hands and feet. You wish you had time to eat your lunch but your mother wants you home. There's packing to do. The past races through your mind, images you'll likely never to forget: the bloody Nile river, croaking frogs, the whiz of whiny locusts, and who could forget the rest of the deadly plagues? Yet today it's freedom that's on your mind!

Your friends, Josiah and Zeb, are up ahead with walking sticks in hand. They are excited about the great escape. And so are you! Let the Egyptians have their many gods. You will place your future in the hands of the God of Israel. Let's give a listen.

The Great Escape
Based on Exodus 12

Two young men clean the mud from their hands and let out shouts of joy!

Josiah: Great news. It's Independence Day!

Zeb: My father just told me that if we follow God's instructions, we'll be free. We're done with slavery!

Josiah: I'm all for that. I'm ready to get out of this town. I'm tired of working for Pharaoh.

Zeb: Me too.

Josiah: I've got even more news to share. Before we go, God wants each family to take a lamb and prepare it for a meal. If your family is too small to eat a whole lamb, you're supposed share it with another. Our families are small enough to share one.

Zeb: Great. What do you want for a side dish? Broccoli? Green bean casserole?

Josiah: According to Moses, God has planned the whole menu.

Zeb: *(takes out a pad and pencil)* Okay, shoot. What's your order?

Josiah: Here are God's instructions. The lamb must be killed at twilight. And not just any lamb will do. It has to be a year-old male in perfect condition.

Zeb: Got it. I'll do it tomorrow, right before lunch.

Josiah: God's instructions tell us it must be done today, Zeb, at twilight, when the sun goes down.

Josiah: *(distracted)* Yeah, yeah I got it. I wonder if good ole Jacob still has that three-footed sheep he got two years ago for his birthday. Daisy was her name and, boy, could she do the two-step! *(dances a jig)*

Josiah: No, no! That sheep's too old. And it has to be a male sheep. M-A-L-E!

Zeb: Picky, picky.

Josiah: Roast the meat over the fire along with bitter herbs and serve bread without yeast.

Zeb: Gotcha, broiled lamb and…

Josiah: Roasted!

Zeb: Roasted lamb, with some salt and pepper and a little nutmeg for flavor. That's my secret ingredient, I add it to everything.

Josiah: No, no! Bitter herbs, you must use bitter herbs. Zeb, are you sure you can handle this?

Zeb: Sure. Broiled lamb with some soft, warm, dinner rolls.

Josiah: Roasted! And the bread must have no yeast. No soft, warm dinner rolls.

Zeb: No yeast? But that would make the bread…flat!

Josiah: That's right. That was God's own instruction to Moses. Now, Zeb, tell me again everything you must do when the sun goes down.

Zeb: Roast a perfect lamb, add the bitter herbs and mix up a batch of bread with no yeast. I'll get right on it first thing *(yawn)* in the morning.

Josiah: Now, now, now! And bring me the lamb's blood.

Zeb: Okay, right away. You're the boss! *(Exits)*

Josiah: *(yells after Zeb)* Be sure to have your shirt tucked in and your shoes on. That's also one of God's specific instructions. We have to be ready to make a run for it.

Zeb: *(enters huffing and puffing with shoes on and a bowl in hand.)* All done, Josiah.

Josiah: *(Takes bowl.)* Wow. You're quick!

Zeb: "Feasts to Go" in five minutes or less. That's my motto.

Josiah: The final plague that God will send is one that Pharaoh cannot ignore. The angel of death will come to take the first born son from any home that does not have the special protection.

Zeb: Special protection?

Josiah: *(Josiah takes the red crepe paper strips from the bowl and holds them up or tapes them to the door.)* Lamb's blood must mark the doorframe of each home where God's people live. When the angel of death sees the blood, it will pass over that house. Following God's instructions will save us.

Jeb pretends to pass out the food and comments about how good the food tastes.

Josiah: Let's be sure to eat all the lamb. Any leftovers will need to be burned.

Zeb: I heard my father say that God wants us to celebrate this day every year so that our children won't forget what God did for us. Today will forever be known as Passover. **Josiah:** *(licks fingers)* That was a fine meal, Zeb. Now we can travel fast and light.

Zeb: Thanks. A person wants to do a good job on such an important meal.

Josiah: Our last meal in Egypt is finished. Everyone get ready. Let's listen while we wait for death to pass overhead.

Have the group sit quietly and listen. You may wish to play special music here to heighten the dramatic effect.

Josiah: We're safe. Praise God. Everyone, the great escape has now begun. To the desert one and all!

Have kids rise and run in a circle or run out the door.

God gave some amazingly specific instructions for this meal, didn't he! If you were a waiter or waitress, would you have gotten the order straight? Let's see!

Toss the four numbered balls to different parts of the room. Bring the kids with the balls to the front one by one and ask these questions. Allow kids to get help from the group if they need it. After each correct answer, let kids drop the ball into a bag.

■ **What did God put on the menu for the Passover Feast?**

■ **Why did it have to be bread without yeast?**

■ **Why was it important that the Hebrews obey God's careful instructions to the letter?**

■ **Why did God want his people to celebrate this feast every year?**

With the Passover Feast God was setting the stage for two events—one that would happen that very night, and one that wouldn't happen for hundreds of years. That very night God would send death with the tenth and final plague on Egypt. Because Pharaoh disobeyed God and refused to free the Israelite slaves, the firstborn son of each family in Egypt would die—including the Pharaoh's son.

Bible Verse

Now choose life, so that you and your children may live and that you may love the Lord your God, listen to his voice, and hold fast to him.
Deuteronomy 30:19–20

But when the angel of death saw the blood of the lamb on the doorposts of the Israelites' homes, he would pass over and no one would be harmed. That's why this feast is called "Passover." And it happened just as God said. The Pharaoh called Moses and Aaron to the palace and said, "Leave." He couldn't get God's people out of Egypt fast enough!

Like the Israelites, in order to receive God's protection, we need to do what he tells us. When you choose to obey God, you choose life! We don't need to sacrifice lambs any more, because Jesus died for us. He became the last sacrifice we would ever need. When you put your faith in Jesus, you're choosing life.

Dismiss kids to their shepherd groups.

2 Shepherd's Spot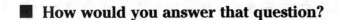

Gather kids in your small group. Help them find Exodus 12 in their Bibles.

God was ready to bring his people out of Egypt. He told them exactly what to do. He wanted them to prepare a meal that would help them remember this night forever.

Invite volunteers to read God's instructions for the Passover Feast from Exodus 12:1–3, 7–8, 12–14, 25–29.

When Jewish people celebrate Passover today, the youngest child at the table always asks, "Why is this night different from all other nights?"

■ **How would you answer that question?**

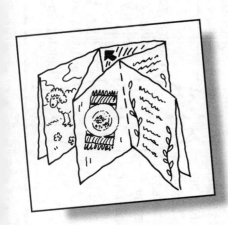

This was the night God would deliver his people from slavery. And it shows us how, hundreds of years later; Jesus would deliver us from sin.

Distribute the "Invitation to a Feast" handout (p. 54). **This booklet shows us what Passover means to people who believe in Jesus.** Lead kids through the following steps.

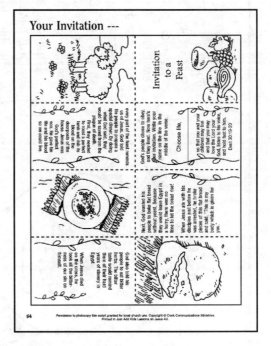

1. Cut out the rectangle on the heavy line.
2. Fold it in half the hamburger way and cut a slit on the line in the middle.
3. Open it, then fold it in half hot dog way. Make creases on all the dotted lines.
4. Holding it folded the hot dog way, push the ends toward the middle. (See the illustration.)
5. Fold the booklet so "Invitation to a Feast" is on the cover and the Bible verse is on the back.

Have kids take turns reading each page of the booklet. Then direct them to the verse on the back cover. **This is your turn to say, "I choose to obey God. I choose life!"** Encourage kids to add their names to the line in the Bible verse.

Invite kids to share their concerns, then close with prayer. **Jesus, we know that you are like the Passover lamb. You gave your life so we can live. Because we know you care for us so much, we pray for** (mention each child's requests). **Help us choose life by obeying you each day, amen.**

Invitation to a Feast

Invitation to a Feast

Every part of the feast reminds us of Jesus. God told his people to prepare a special dinner. By doing what God said, they would be saved from the plague of death.

First, they needed to roast a perfect lamb and dab its blood on the doorposts of the house. Jesus was God's perfect son. He gave his life and his blood so we could live.

God's people chose to obey, and they lived. Now here's your invitation. Write your name on the line in the middle of the verse.

Choose life, _____ so that you and your children may live and that you may love the Lord your God, listen to his voice, and hold fast to him. Deuteronomy 30:19-20

Next, God wanted his people to bake flat bread without yeast. Because they would leave Egypt in a hurry, there was no time to let the bread rise!

When Jesus ate with his disciples just before he was arrested, he broke pieces of this flat bread and said, "This is my body which is given for you."

When Jesus died on the cross, he took all the bitterness of our sin on himself.

God also told his people to eat bitter herbs. The bitter taste would remind them of their hard years of slavery in Egypt.

Recipe 1!

Have you ever tasted a food that reminded you of a special time of year? Pause for kids to respond. **Well, God knows that food and other symbols are a good way to remember things. Food pretty much helps the memory along! Today's Bible story tells us about the first Feast of the Passover. God instructed his people to have a Passover Feast every year as a way of remembering how the death "passed over" their homes as they prepared to flee Egypt. Let's make a fruit dish called** *Haroseth* **that's often served at Passover time. This memory food serves as a reminder to God's people of the mortar the Israelites used to build Pharaoh's cities.**

Core apples. Have kids use knives to cut the apples into cubes.

> ■ **How does all this chopping remind the Hebrew people of life in Egypt?** (The Israelites endured many years of hard work.)

Mix all remaining ingredients. Add sugar to taste. Serve. (Makes about 8 cups of fruit.)

The Israelites lived in Egypt a long, long time—430 years! (Exodus 12:40) When they finally left the country headed for the desert it's estimated that there were nearly two million strong. The Israelites would continue to honor their Creator for generations by obeying his direction and celebrating this, the Seder or Passover meal.

> ■ **In what ways might you have celebrated God's ticket to freedom?**

Get List:
- ❏ plastic knives or fruit chopper
- ❏ bowl
- ❏ napkins
- ❏ serving cups and spoons

Passover Haroseth
8 apples
2/3 cup chopped almonds
4 Tbsp. grape juice
3 Tbsp. sugar or to taste
1 tsp. cinnamon
grated rind of 1 lemon

Recipe 2!

This sweet treat is made with matzo. Matzo is the "bread" without yeast that God required the Israelites to eat at Passover. It's known as unleavened bread and tastes something like unsalted crackers.

Get List:
- ❏ matzo crackers
- ❏ quick hardening chocolate syrup
- ❏ wax paper
- ❏ cookie tray
- ❏ crushed nuts

Break off pieces of matzo for each child. Place the matzo on individual pieces of wax paper. Have the kids take turns drizzling quick-hardening chocolate shell onto the flat bread. Sprinkle with crushed nuts. Place the chocolate covered matzos on a cookie sheet or tray and place in the refrigerator for about five minutes. The treats will harden quickly.

> ■ **God's people ate the Passover Feast while dressed in their traveling clothes. What does this say about their faith and trust in God's promises?**

> ■ **The Hebrews followed God's Word and they were given life and freedom. How does this remind you of Jesus' death on the cross and the life and freedom we have in him?**

Following God's instructions brought freedom to the Israelites. But it also kept their firstborn sons alive. Unfortunately, Egyptians cries told a different story. Today, we read the Bible because God's Word brings us life, joy, comfort and peace of mind. Let's live with its wisdom and protection.

Fold down the corners to start your paper airplane.

SPECIAL DELIVERY

TO

Follow God's Word.

Today at church we heard how God led his people out of Egypt.

° Why did the Israelites want to leave Egypt?

° Tell your family what you learned about the Feast of the Passover.

The Israelites couldn't wait to leave Egypt. After hundreds of years of slavery, they longed to be free—and with God's help they made it! Ask permission to borrow a silk tie or scarf from mom or dad. Rub the silk on the inside and outside of a clean glass for two minutes. Now tear tissue paper into small pieces and sprinkle it over the glass. Watch. At first, the paper will stick to the glass. Then just as suddenly the pieces will flee from it!

Bible Verse

Now choose life, so that you and your children may live and that you may love the Lord your God, listen to his voice, and hold fast to him.
Deuteronomy 30:19–20

◊ Passover is a Jewish holiday.
What holidays do Christians celebrate as a reminder of God's love and his Son's sacrifice?

☆ Family FUN ☆

Live It!

Cross on the Red

Get Set
LARGE GROUP ■ Greet kids and do a puppet skit. Schooner talks about flying free in God's care.

❏ large bird puppet ❏ puppeteer

1

Bible 4U! Instant Drama
LARGE GROUP ■ Moses' very own sandals banter the pros and cons of crossing the Red Sea.

❏ 2 actors ❏ copies of pp. 60–61, Saving Soles script ❏ 4 numbered balls ❏ bag
Optional: ❏ 2 Bibletime costumes

2

Shepherd's Spot
SMALL GROUP ■ Use a handout to "make waves" to represent the walls of water the Israelites walked through. Share concerns and pray together. Send home the Special Delivery handout.

❏ Bibles ❏ scissors ❏ glue stick ❏ copies of p. 64, Crossing the Red Sea
❏ copies of p. 66, Special Delivery

Workshop Wonders
SMALL GROUP ■ Fun and simple activities lead into a God-will-make-a-way experiment.

❏ 4 juggling balls (used in Bible 4U!) ❏ hard-sided books ❏ spoons
❏ hardboiled egg(s) ❏ glass bottle (iced tea or coffee-drink bottle) ❏ matches
Optional: ❏ long wooden skewer

Bible Basis
The Exodus and Crossing the Red Sea Exodus 12:31–32; 14:8,13–14, 19–22, 26–27, 31; 15:1–2

Learn It!
God will make a way.

Live It!
Rejoice in God's care.

Bible Verse
The Lord is my strength and my song; he has become my salvation. Exodus 15:2

Quick Takes

Exodus 12:31–32; 14:8,13–14, 19–22, 26–27, 31; 15:1–2

During the night Pharaoh summoned Moses and Aaron and said, "Up! Leave my people, you and the Israelites! Go, worship the Lord as you have requested.

32 Take your flocks and herds, as you have said, and go. And also bless me."

14:8 The Lord hardened the heart of Pharaoh king of Egypt, so that he pursued the Israelites, who were marching out boldly.

13 Moses answered the people, "Do not be afraid. Stand firm and you will see the deliverance the Lord will bring you today. The Egyptians you see today you will never see again.

14 The Lord will fight for you; you need only to be still."

19 Then the angel of God, who had been travelling in front of Israel's army, withdrew and went behind them. The pillar of cloud also moved from in front and stood behind them,

20 coming between the armies of Egypt and Israel. Throughout the night the cloud brought darkness to the one side and light to the other; so neither went near the other all night long.

21 Then Moses stretched out his hand over the sea, and all that night the Lord drove the sea back with a strong east wind and turned it into dry land. The waters were divided,

22 and the Israelites went through the sea on dry ground, with a wall of water on their right and on their left.

26 Then the Lord said to Moses, "Stretch out your hand over the sea so that the waters may flow back over the Egyptians and their chariots and horsemen."

27 Moses stretched out his hand over the sea, and at daybreak the sea went back to its place. The Egyptians were fleeing towards it, and the Lord swept them into the sea.

31 And when the Israelites saw the great power the Lord displayed against the Egyptians, the people feared the Lord and put their trust in him and in Moses his servant.

15:1 Then Moses and the Israelites sang this song to the Lord: "I will sing to the Lord, for he is highly exalted. The horse and its rider he has hurled into the sea.

2 The Lord is my strength and my song; he has become my salvation. He is my God, and I will praise him, my father's God, and I will exalt him."

Insights

This is it. The Israelites are on their way. The death of all the firstborn sons of Egypt convinced Pharaoh to give up his struggle with God.

Have you ever had to rush off in the middle of the night? To a hospital, an emergency plane flight, to the deathbed of a beloved family member? A quick exit in the dark brings a rush of adrenaline and no small amount of fear.

Think of all the things that were about to change. They were leaving their homes, taking the possessions they could carry. They were a whole nation–more than a million people–on foot.

Daylight comes and they're still pressing on into the desert. Then they feel it. The trembling of the earth that means only one thing: horses' hooves pounding the sand. In terror they realize that Pharaoh's army is on its way. They're doomed.

But God had saved them from all manner of calamities in Egypt. Would he save them again?

As the milling crowds start to panic, Moses cries out to God. Following God's instructions he holds his staff over the sea. Walls of water rise as the sea parts. Hurry! God has made a way!

The youngest and the oldest shuffle across the miraculous path as quickly as their legs can carry them. The chariots aren't far behind. Then Moses lowers his staff and the sea swallows the enemy. Imagine the loudest cheer you've ever heard at a sporting event. Now put more than a million people into that cheer. Let the celebration begin!

God has a wonderful habit of making a way for his people when they hit hopeless dead ends. Share this great news with your kids and encourage their faith in our incredible living God.

 **Get Set**

Go-o-o-o-d morning! Thanks for being here. We have some exciting things for you today, so let's get started. Hmm...isn't there supposed to be a bird around here somewhere? *Schooner pops up.*

Schooner: Ta da!
Leader: Hello, Schooner.

Schooner: Hello!
Leader: Let's start things off a little different.

Schooner: How's that?
Leader: I'll ask you, What's up?

Schooner: Flying is what's up.
Leader: Flying. I get it!

Schooner: I'm talking about flying the coop.
Leader: Tell us more, Schooner.

Schooner: I wasn't always a free bird, you know.
Leader: No?

Schooner: I spent some hard time in a very nice pet shop.
Leader: A pet shop, you say?

Schooner: But there was lots to eat.
Leader: That's good.

Schooner: And fresh water every day.
Leader: Better yet.

Schooner: And it was there that I learned my very first words.
Leader: You've learned quite a few since then, Schooner.

Schooner: I like to squawk. *Squawk!*
Leader: We're happy you do.

Schooner: Anyway, a cage is not a happy place for a bird.
Leader: So I hear.

Schooner: One day the cage door opened.
Leader: And...

Schooner: ...the pet shop door did too.
Leader: And away you went!

Schooner: Bye, bye birdie!
Leader: And the rest, as they say, is history.

Schooner: Safe and sound and here with you and all these fine folks.
Leader: Then you know a little about how God's people felt.

Schooner: Freedom! I'm glad God's people got to finally leave Egypt.
Leader: Free after hundreds of years.

Schooner: Something tells me that's not the whole story, boss.
Leader: Pharaoh did let God's people go.

Schooner: But?
Leader: ...but not for long.

Schooner: What?!?
Leader: The Pharaoh wanted them back.

Schooner: This Pharaoh is getting on my nerves.
Leader: Pharaoh sent his armies and chariots and best swordsmen to make sure the Israelites returned.

Schooner: No way!
Leader: But there's more to the story.

Schooner: Tell me it gets better.
Leader: Oh, it does! God made a way for his people to remain free.

Schooner: Whew! That's good news.
Leader: And it had something to do with a sea.

Schooner: *(sings) by the sea*
Leader: *(joins in) by the sea*
Leader and Schooner: *(sing together) by the beautiful sea!*

Leader: God performs an amazing sea miracle so his people can get away.

Schooner: So spill the beans, boss!
Leader: Think walls of water.

Schooner: *(muses)* Wall of water...hey, like the waves at Wave World?
Leader: Great idea, Schooner! You know how the water rises then falls in the wave pool?

Schooner: Sure.
Leader: Well, God does something like that to a whole body of water called the Red Sea.

Schooner: It was red?
Leader: No, but it had lots of reeds. Think of reeds as tall water weeds.

Schooner: So with walls of water God made a way.
Leader: God's people sang and rejoiced that day.

Schooner: *(looks to the group)* More for you and me in Bible 4U!

1 Bible 4U!

It's time for another Bible 4U! theater. Today's story takes place on the shore of the Red Sea. Moses leads the people of Israel through the wilderness to a life of freedom. You might recall that God commanded Pharaoh, the king of Egypt, to let the Israelites leave Egypt. But, Pharaoh did not want to lose his free help. So, God sent ten devastating plagues upon Pharaoh and the Egyptian people. Finally, the Pharaoh let God's people leave his rule.

Instant Prep

Before class, ask two strong readers to play the roles of Moses' sandals. Give both readers copies of the "Saving Soles" script below.

But once again this fickle Pharaoh changed his mind. He realized the cost of all that free help now fleeing through his fingers. With chariots and men on horseback, Pharaoh's soldiers chased the Israelites to drag them back to Egypt.

for Overachievers

Make 2 large cardboard shoeprints. Label one Sandal #1 and the second Sandal #2. Attach a string to the shoe pairs and give one set to each actor to drape from the neck or shoulders.

In today's Bible 4U! we find the Israelites camped out at the Red Sea. Imagine going on a camping trip with almost two million people! Everyone's excited and just a little scared. After all, they've never been free before! But now a sea blocks their way. I wonder what they'll do when they hear the wheels of Pharaoh's chariots? Look! Here comes a pair of sandals. They belong to Moses. Let's listen.

Saving Soles
Based on Exodus 12–15

Sandal 1: *(In a tired and whiny voice)* I can't believe this. All this walking, and we've hit a watery dead end. Look at this! Miles of water.

Sandal 2: Maybe it's shallow enough to wade through. *(Leans forward as if to try)*

Sandal 1: *(shocked)* Are you nuts? Get back here. *(grabs Sandal 2 and pulls him/her back)* You don't want to get wet—because I don't want to get wet! Our leather would get ruined for sure. Moses would throw us away with yesterday's trash.

Sandal 2: Don't be silly. We are Moses' number one sandals. He'll be wearing us until the day he dies.

Sandal 1: Speak for yourself. I intend to retire early. I've earned it with all this walking in the desert. How much further do we have to go anyway?

Sandal 2: I don't know. We just have to trust God to take care of us. After all, he convinced Pharaoh to let the Israelites go.

Sandal 1: And look where we are now! Stuck in the desert with no way around this huge body of stupid water. *(Gives the water a swift kick.)*

Sandal 2: Hush! That's no way for a prophet's sandal to speak.

Sandal 1: *(grumbles)* Sorry.

Sandal 2: Tighten your straps and have faith. God will make a way. Look how he sent a pillar of cloud to guard us. *(Points to the sky.)* It separates us from the army of Egypt and gives us all the light we need.

Sandal 1: The army of Egypt? When did they show up? Good grief—they're going to capture us and take us back to Egypt!

Sandal 2: Oh, no they won't! Look, Moses is stretching his hand over the sea, and the water's moving. It's bunching up and separating. How awesome is that!

Sandal 1: That wind is strong. But do you think we can cross? Listen, I don't want to get out there, get stuck in the mud, and have those walls of water spring a leak!

Sandal 2: Don't worry. God will take you and me and all the people here.

Sandal 1: Brrr. The last thing I need is water stains.

Sandal 2: The Lord is our strength. Rising water will not change that.

Sandal 1 and 2 begin walking in place. Sandal 1 keeps looking to the left and right, as if he is unsure if the water will hold. Sandal 2 looks straight ahead and walks confidently.

Sandal 1: *(with a worried look)* This is scary. I wonder what's going on behind us. Hey, look over here! Seaweed and cute little fish. Come here, little fishie, fishie, fishie. *(Extends hand to pet fish.)*

Sandal 2: *(quickly)* Um, I wouldn't waste time. The Egyptian army is on our heels.

Sandal 1: *(panics and pulls hand back)* Yikes! *(hysterical)* Everybody, hold on to your soles and run for your lives! Run for your LIVES!

Sandal 1 grabs hold of Sandal 2. Both sandals stop walking in place.

Sandal 2: Quiet now. Look. We're on dry ground.

Sandal 1: *(sighs in relief)* Feels great. But I hate squishy toes.

Sandal 2: God is on our side. The last Israelite has crossed and God is releasing the walls of water.

Sandal 1: *(looks back and squints)* The Egyptian soldiers and their horses and, yes, their chariots, cannot escape. Going once, going twice, swallowed up by the sea! *(Sticks out a leather tongue and in a sing-song voice says...)* Nah, nah, nah, nah, nah, nah! You can't get us!

Sandal 2: Enough of that. You don't have to be nasty about it.

Sandal 1: We're free! We're free! And on dry ground. That silly ole' Pharaoh can't get us now.

Sandal 2: Do you hear that? People are singing. They're rejoicing in God's care. Let's join in!

Sandal 1: *(sings in full operatic voice) If I had a hammer, I'd hammer in the mor-or-ning.*

Sandal 2: Wrong song.

Sandal 1: Oops.

Sandal 2: Listen to the group, silly.

Sandal 1: *(clears throat and starts marching.)* I will sing to the Lord, for he is highly exalted. The horse and its rider he has hurled into the sea. Yes, sir!

Sandal 2: The Lord is my strength and my song; he has become my salvation.

Sandal 1: Hey—now the people are singing and dancing with joy!

Sandal 2: We can get into that. Left foot leads, right foot cha...cha...chas!

Free at last! Free at last! Hear the shouts from God's people as they flee Egypt. But fear was soon to follow them. The Israelites had run for their lives into the desert only to face a body of water that meant death—either by drowning or an Egyptian sword. Ready for the great ball toss? Grab one if it comes your way.

Toss the four numbered balls to different parts of the room. Bring the kids with the balls to the front one-by-one and ask these questions. Allow kids to get help from the group if they need it. After each correct answer, let kids drop the ball into a bag.

■ Why were Moses' sandals afraid in today's drama?

■ If you were one of the sandals in today's story, would you trust God enough to get your toes wet? Why or why not?

■ How did God make a way in what seemed to be an impossible situation?

■ How did the Israelites celebrate God's help?

I think Moses' sandals in our story were pretty smart. If I were in their shoes, I'd want to have God on my side too!

Imagine your thoughts as the greatest army of its day thundered and roared towards you and your family. Fear must have grabbed the hearts of God's men, women and children. Thankfully, God would not leave his people to die near a sea's muddy shore. He had big plans for them, plans of love and life, not sorrow and death.

Even if the Israelites could not see the big picture, God's could. His power would provide safe passage through—not around—the Red Sea. And as the walls of water fell, Pharaoh's horses, chariots and finest soldiers were washed into the sea. Pharaoh's power was no match for the forces of our one and only God.

Bible Verse
The Lord is my strength and my song; he has become my salvation.
Exodus 15:2

Dismiss kids to their shepherd groups.

2 Shepherd's Spot

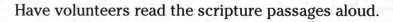

Gather your small group and help them find Exodus 12 in the Bibles. If you have sticky notes, help them mark these passages: Exodus 12:31–32; 14:8, 13–14, 19–22, 26–27, 31; 15:1–2.

Wow. This is exciting stuff! Earth-shaking, heart-pounding, nerve-rattling adventure. The Israelites are on their way out of Egypt. But it's out of the frying pan and into the water! Let's read it straight from God's Word.

Have volunteers read the scripture passages aloud.

■ **If you had the opportunity to be there, would you take it? Why or why not?**

The Israelites were at a watery dead end with the enemy closing fast, but God was just getting warmed up! Sometimes we hit dead ends in our lives, and we don't see anyway out.

■ **What do those dead ends in life look like?**

Good news! God can make a way for you just as he did for the Israelites. When God is in the picture, there's no such thing as a dead end!

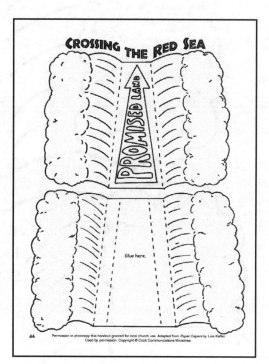

Share a personal experience of God making a way for you when you seemed to be at a dead end. Then distribute the "Crossing the Red Sea" handouts. Lead kids through these assembly steps.

1. Cut the sections apart on the heavy outlines.
2. Fold in on the dotted lines. Roll the edges of the waves around smooth pencils so they curve, creating walls of water.
3. Glue the smaller section inside the larger one.

Maybe you know someone who seems to be at a dead end. Let's pray for those people. Let kids share their concerns, then close with prayer. **Heavenly Father, you are truly amazing. We love to hear how you made a way for your people. We pray that you'll make a way for** (name people the kids mentioned). **Please make a way for them. In Jesus' name, amen.**

CROSSING THE RED SEA

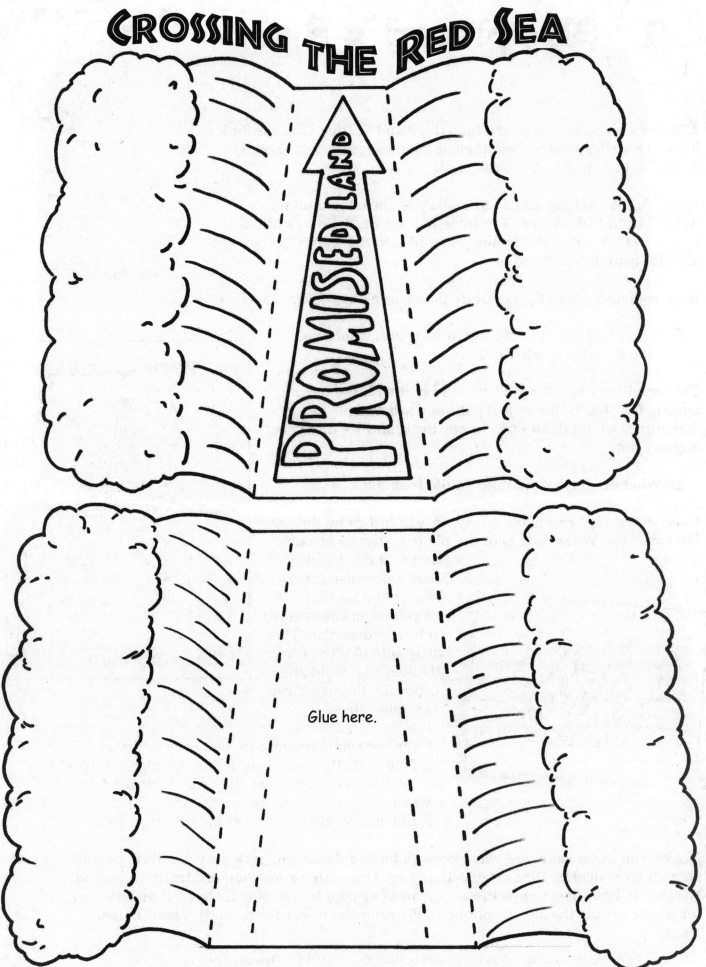

PROMISED LAND

Glue here.

Workshop Wonders

Today I need your help with some fun activities. If you'd like to volunteer, be sure to raise your hand. Here goes! Who can balance a book on their head while walking across the room? From your volunteers, choose both girls and boys.

Good job! Now, I need volunteers who can balance a spoon on the nose and walk across the room. Again, ask volunteers to come up. Choose different kids each time so everyone gets a turn.

What talent! Now, who can roll their tongue like a hot dog? Do the wave with your eyebrows? Have all kids give both of these a try. **Awesome! Now I need a juggler.** Start out your volunteer with two balls, then add a third and a fourth.

Juggling four balls is difficult but not impossible. You may have seen it done by a professional juggler. Okay. Here's is my last teaser. Can anyone come up with a way to get this hard-boiled egg into this glass bottle without cutting or smashing the egg?

Get List:
- ❏ 4 juggling balls
- ❏ hard-sided books
- ❏ spoons
- ❏ hardboiled egg(s)
- ❏ glass bottle (an iced tea or coffee-drink bottle works well)
- ❏ matches

Optional:
- ❏ wooden skewer

While kids share their answers, begin peeling the hardboiled egg. **It seems impossible to get the egg inside the bottle without damaging it. But, I have a way.** Light three matches, one at a time, and drop them into the bottle. Then, have a child place the hardboiled egg in the mouth of the jar. Poof! The matches will go out immediately. As the smoke rises the egg will slowly suck into the bottle. (If you have a church with sensitive smoke detectors, you might want to take this activity outside.) If you brought extra hardboiled eggs let kids try their hand at the experiment. Use a wooden skewer to break the egg inside the bottle into smaller pieces and discard before another student steps up to give it a try.

■ **Many of you thought it was impossible to get the egg into the bottle without breaking it. The Israelites in today's Bible story thought they had an impossible situation too. What was it?**

Air pressure is what it's all about. The heated air inside the bottle cools and contracts when the matches finally burn down. This creates lower air pressure inside the bottle than outside The greater pressure forces the egg to do its thing!

■ **How did God make a way for them to cross the Red Sea? What happened to the Egyptian army close behind?**

■ **Share a time when you thought something was impossible but later realized God had made a way for you or your family.**

With respect and trust in their hearts, the Israelites sang a song of joy to honor God, who accomplished the impossible to save them from the Egyptian sword. God will make a way. And nothing—not chariots, armies or muddy sea bottoms—will stop his plan. Rejoice and trust in God's care!

Fold down the corners to start your paper airplane.

SPECIAL DELIVERY

TO

Rejoice in God's care.

Today at church we heard about the Exodus and the Red Sea: How do you think the Israelites felt when the Red Sea was crossing? When have you felt trapped in an impossible situation? How did God help you?

Next time it's tub time think of the Red Sea! Before you get into the tub mix a colorful paint using 1/2 cup of liquid hand soap and 1 tsp. of cornstarch. Add a few drops of red food coloring to the mixture. With the tub as your canvas draw a wavy Red Sea, or write one or two colorful keywords that highlight today's Bible story, such as: Lord, Moses, desert, cloud, army, angel, hand, water, trust. Be sure to scrub the tub and the wall with cleanser once your bath is through.

Bible Verse

The Lord is my strength and my song; he has become my salvation.
Exodus 15:2

◊ Suppose you were with the Israelites that crossed the Red Sea. How would you explain it to someone who didn't see it happen?

◊ What would you do the moment you saw the sea swallow the Egyptian army?

66 ☆ Family FUN ☆

Live It!

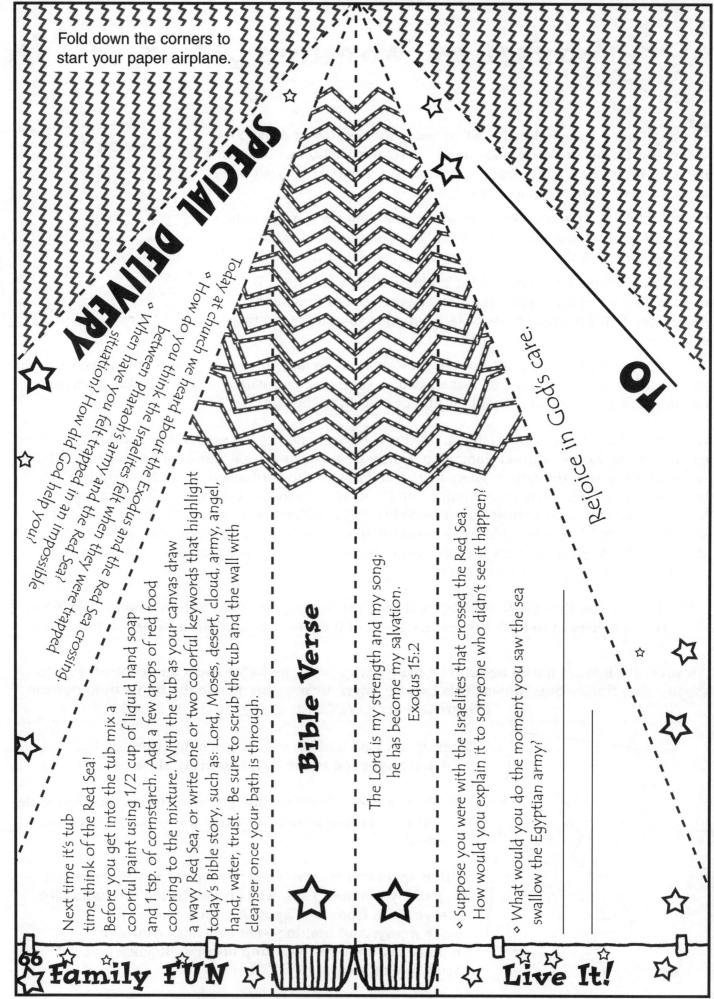

Fast Food in the Desert

Get Set
Option

LARGE GROUP ■ Greet kids and do a puppet skit. A hungry Schooner learns of the Israelites need for food and water in today's story.

❏ large bird puppet ❏ puppeteer

Bible 4U! Instant Drama
1

LARGE GROUP ■ A storyteller's clever rhyme speaks of desert-weary travelers tired of manna.

❏ 1 young storyteller ❏ copy of pp. 70–71, Mumble, Grumble, Gripe and Groan rhyme ❏ 4 numbered balls ❏ bag Optional: ❏ Bibletime costumes

Shepherd's Spot
2

SMALL GROUP ■ Make a basket to collect things that remind you of God's care. Share concerns and pray. Send home the Special Delivery handout.

❏ Bibles ❏ pencils ❏ scissors ❏ glue sticks ❏ copies of p. 74, Manna Basket ❏ copies of p. 76, Special Delivery

Workshop Wonders
Option

SMALL GROUP ■ Brown and white fun foam come together in a bread-shaped magnet for the home that will remind kids of manna. Bread 'n' butter provides a yummy snack while kids work.

❏ scissors ❏ white glue ❏ pens ❏ white fun foam ❏ brown fun foam ❏ magnet strips or rolls ❏ wet wipes. Optional: ❏ scrap paper ❏ slices of rye bread ❏ pencils ❏ honey butter

Bible Basis
Food and water in the desert.
Exodus 16:2–3, 11–16, 35; 17:1–6

Learn It!
God takes care of our needs.

Live It!
Look to God for your needs.

Bible Verse
The Lord will guide you always; he will satisfy your needs.
Isaiah 58:11

Quick Takes

Exodus 16:2–3, 11–16, 35; 17:1–6

In the desert the whole community grumbled against Moses and Aaron. The Israelites said to them, "If only we had died by the Lord's hand in Egypt! There we sat round pots of meat and ate all the food we wanted, but you have brought us out into this desert to starve this entire assembly to death." 16:2-3

16:11-16 The Lord said to Moses, "I have heard the grumbling of the Israelites. Tell them, 'At twilight you will eat meat, and in the morning you will be filled with bread. Then you will know that I am the Lord your God.'" That evening quail came and covered the camp, and in the morning there was a layer of dew around the camp. When the dew was gone, thin flakes like frost on the ground appeared on the desert floor. When the Israelites saw it, they said to each other, "What is it?" For they did not know what it was. Moses said to them, "It is the bread the Lord has given you to eat. This is what the Lord has commanded: 'Each one is to gather as much as he needs. Take an omer for each person you have in your tent.'"

16:35 The Israelites ate manna for forty years, until they came to a land that was settled; they ate manna until they reached the border of Canaan

17:1-6 The whole Israelite community set out from the Desert of Sin, travelling from place to place as the Lord commanded. They camped at Rephidim, but there was no water for the people to drink. So they quarreled with Moses and said, "Give us water to drink." Moses replied, "Why do you quarrel with me? Why do you put the Lord to the test?" But the people were thirsty for water there, and they grumbled against Moses. They said, "Why did you bring us up out of Egypt to make us and our children and livestock die of thirst?" Then Moses cried out to the Lord, "What am I to do with these people? They are almost ready to stone me." The Lord answered Moses, "Walk on ahead of the people. Take with you some of the elders of Israel and take in your hand the staff with which you struck the Nile, and go. I will stand there before you by the rock at Horeb. Strike the rock, and water will come out of it for the people to drink." So Moses did this in the sight of the elders of Israel.

Insights

More than a million and a half-hungry, thirsty people are on foot. The terrain is barren, with a few oases scattered miles apart. The face of survival has changed from escaping to finding food and water for a nation traveling through a dry and thirsty land.

These people have been slaves their whole lives. They've been told what to do, driven hard year after year. Suddenly they're free. They're faced choices and decisions they've never had to make before. The exhilaration of freedom is sobered by bewilderment. All that's familiar is gone, literally overnight. Egypt was a wealthy nation where even the slaves probably ate well. They'd enjoyed seafood, meat and an abundance of fresh fruit and vegetables. The frightened Israelites wondered if they'd escaped the clutches of Pharaoh only to die of starvation.

God spent the next forty years teaching his people to rely on him daily for their needs—twice daily, in fact. When they woke in the morning, they found manna on the ground. In the evening, quail flew into the camp. So that they would never forget, God instructed the Israelites to keep an omer (a little more than two quarts) in a pot, which was later placed in the Ark of the Covenant with the tablets containing the Ten Commandments.

Jesus reminded his disciples of the "daily-ness" of trusting God for what we need. He taught them to pray, "Give us today our daily bread." This is perhaps a harder lesson for adults than for children. These lessons of trusting God as our provider need to start young so that children's minds are molded by God's truth, not by society. Use this lesson to help kids understand that God wants them to look to him as their Abba—their daddy—who loves them more than they will ever know.

68

Option Get Set

Hey—is anybody hungry? Did anybody miss breakfast this morning? You look like a pretty well fed group. Fortunately, you have a fridge at home and some food in the cupboard. It wasn't like that for the Israelites. Schooner, hop up here and help me share the story. *Schooner "hops" up.*

Schooner: *(Schooner makes two gigantic hops)* How's that for hopping?

Leader: Very good.

Schooner: Really?

Leader: With long ears you'd make a great bunny.

Schooner: Never!

Leader: A little joke, Schooner.

Schooner: Oh, oh.

Leader: What is it, Schooner? My joke wasn't that bad.

Schooner: It's my tummy, boss.

Leader: *(alarmed)* Should I call the doctor…I mean, vet?

Schooner: *(leans on Leader)* No. I've had this before. I know the cure.

Leader: We'll get whatever you need, Schooner.

Schooner: *(breathes heavy)* Got a pencil for the number?

Leader: I have a great memory. Shoot.

Schooner: *(sounds faint)* Call…

Leader: Yes?

Schooner: Call…for a…

Leader: Yes? Yes?

Schooner: an anchovy and cheese pizza with fresh pineapple. *Stat!*

Leader: *(gently nudges Schooner upright)* Wait a minute. I thought…

Schooner: All that hopping made me hungry, boss.

Leader: But you only hopped twice!

Schooner: It's a medical fact that parrots that hop burn more calories than bunnies that don't.

Leader: *(shakes head)* Where did you read that?

Schooner: In the PMAJ.

Leader: Ok. I'll bite. What's the PMAJ?

Schooner: The Parrots Medical Association Journal.

Leader: Ah.

Schooner: So how about that pizza?

Leader: Hold the phone, Schooner. Let's talk about God's people and their need for food in today's Bible story.

Schooner: Did they feel woozy like me?

Leader: Hot and grumpy was more like it. And they let Moses know it.

Schooner: Lack of pizza can do that to a person…and to a parrot. *Squawk!*

Leader: *(wipes hand)* Schooner, you're drooling!

Schooner: Sorry, boss.

Leader: Getting back to the Bible story…

Schooner: I'm all cheese…I mean ears!

Leader: As I was saying, traveling in the desert from place to place made the Israelites hungry and thirsty.

Schooner: I can relate!

Leader: But God took care of his people's needs.

Schooner: So what was on the menu?

Leader: Think of it as take-out, Schooner.

Schooner: I'll buy that.

Leader: An all-you-can-eat special.

Schooner: Watch out, tummy. Here comes the grub! Here comes the grub!

Leader: God provided his people with the bread and water they needed for their long journey in the sun.

Schooner: Sounds sweet. *(starts hopping again)*

Leader: Now what are you doing?

Schooner: I'm keeping my mind off food.

Leader: While you're hopping remember that God loves us. He'll take care of our needs too.

Schooner: *(still hopping)* Right, boss.

Leader: And not only food and water. God promises to guide us in his ways.

Schooner: *(hops madly)* Waaaterrrrr! I need water!

Leader: Now you sound just like an Israelite, Schooner.

Schooner: *(out of breath)* Time for Bible 4U! *Stat!*

1 Bible 4U!

Bible 4U! coming on through! Today I'd like you to imagine you're at home in your kitchen. It's close to dinnertime. And your tummy grumbles You open the cupboard to find—there's nothing to eat. Week-old hamburger buns will just not cut it.

The Israelites weren't in kitchens but in their tents in the desert. They were hungry too. And thirsty. But in the middle of a desert there aren't many places to go food shopping.

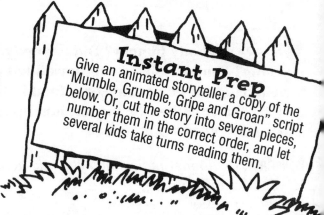

Instant Prep

Give an animated storyteller a copy of the "Mumble, Grumble, Gripe and Groan" script below. Or, cut the story into several pieces, number them in the correct order, and let several kids take turns reading them.

for Overachievers

Have a drama team prepare the script. Use one storyteller dressed in a Bibletime costume. Dress the rest of the actors in black and give them boxes of frosted corn cereal. When the storyteller says, "Let's eat!" let them sprinkle a few flakes into the cupped hands of listeners. Give them clean squirt bottles so they can squirt water in kids' mouths when the storyteller yells, "Slurp!"

Yet, God provided the Israelites with what they needed—water and food in the form of manna. Moses called manna bread from the Lord. (Exodus 16:15) Each morning, except the last day of the week, manna fell like snow in small white flakes. Think of frosted flakes falling from heaven! God's people gathered it off the ground and ate it.

Sounds good, huh? How about eating it day in and day out for 40 years! Let's listen as the Israelites complain of yet another manna meal.

Mumble, Grumble, Gripe and Groan
Based on Exodus 16–17

Mumble, grumble, gripe and groan.
Whine and wail and cry and moan.
Every day we get more manna.
Never figs or ripe bananas.
Gimme dates or mutton stew.
Anything unique would do.
No-more-manna!

Manna dumplings, manna pie.
Manna muffins, my oh my!
Nothing else around to buy.
   Manna stir-fried, manna boiled
     Manna baked and flaked and broiled.
     And overnight the manna's spoiled!
     No-more-manna!

Manna salad, manna cake.
The thought gives me a stomachache.
How much more can one kid take?
I've even had some manna tea
Though we're quite far from the sea.
(A little joke there—pardon me.)*
No-more-manna!

The manna menu's such a bore
I can't take it anymore.
I wish we had a grocery store.
What's a kid like me to do
When the options are so few?
I'd like a steak to barbecue.
No-more-manna!

BUT:
Back before the manna fell
Things weren't going all that well.
Every day our stomachs growled
Toddlers fussed and babies howled.
We would starve—that's what we feared.
We prayed and then this food appeared!

Let's eat!

The Lord Jehovah heard our prayer.
Then—manna, manna everywhere.
Every day each family takes
Baskets full of frosted flakes
"It tastes like honey-flavored bread!"
That's what Uncle Eli said.

It's God who makes the manna fall
Or else we'd have no food at all.
That would be ca-TAS-trophal!
Trusting God's the thing to do
He sends flocks of quail, too.
Perhaps I'll have some manna stew.
Thank you, Lord, for manna.

Let's eat!

A few days later:
Mumble, grumble, gripe and groan.
Whine and wail and cry and moan.
What a huge no-water zone!
I want a drink!

We thought Egypt was the worst
But now we're scared we'll die of thirst.
We'll get rid of Moses first.
I want a drink!

I'm so thirsty I could choke.
I know I'll shrivel up and croak.
This Moses guy is such a joke!
I want a drink!

He led us through the sea, it's true
And washed up Pharaoh's army too.
It was an awesome thing to do, but
I want a drink!

Life right now is no big treat.
Sweaty people, tired feet.
Dragging through the desert heat.
I want a drink!

Where is God? What is his plan?
This desert's like a frying pan!
I thought Moses was the man.
I want a drink!

He's our leader. It's his task.
To give me water for my flask;
Is that so very much to ask?
I want a drink!

Moses has his miracle rod,
The very one he got from God.
The one that left old Pharaoh awed.
Will I get a drink?

He's using it to hit a rock.
Water's gushing! What a shock!
This is *not* the time to talk.
God sent a drink!

Slurp!

I'm beginning to understand
That God has everything all planned
As we cross this barren land.
Thanks for the drink.

God wants us to travel light
Knowing things will be all right
Because he's with us day and night.
I'll trust you, Lord. (I think.)

*A "manatee" is a sea cow.

Anybody hungry for a little heavenly bread and some roasted quail? I hope you gathered lots of great thoughts about how God takes care of us from this story. Let's check out what you've learned.

Toss the four numbered balls to different parts of the room. Bring the kids with the balls to the front one-by-one and ask these questions. Allow kids to get help from the group if they need it. After each correct answer, let kids drop the ball into a bag.

 ■ **Do you every gripe about being hungry? Thirsty? What's your number one "gripe-about" food that makes you groan every time it appears on the table?**

 ■ **Why did God set things up so the people had to pick up their food day by day instead of giving them a big supply at once?**

 ■ **Name five things you believe God will provide for you every day.**

 ■ **You can't see God. Does that make it easier or harder for you to trust him? Explain.**

It's pretty easy to sit here with tummies full of Cheerios® and orange juice and corn flakes and think, what was wrong with those Israelites anyway? Why didn't they remember all the miracles God did to help them escape from Egypt? Did they really think God would just let them die of hunger and thirst?

Most kids in our country have plenty to eat. And all we have to do to get a nice, cool drink is turn on the faucet. Things weren't so easy for a million people wandering in the desert. Every morning and every night, they got their food straight from the hand of God. God set things up that way so he could send his people a big message: " TRUST ME!"

Bible Verse
The Lord will guide you always; he will satisfy your needs.
Isaiah 58:11

That message us for us too. Sometimes, when things are good, it's pretty easy to trust God. In fact, we might not even think about it. But God wants us to think about it! Today in your shepherd groups you'll think about all the wonderful things God gives us every single day.

Dismiss kids to their small groups.

2 Shepherd's Spot

Gather your small group. Help kids find Exodus 16 in their Bibles.

Have you ever been stuck on a long trip with no food in the car and no place to stop and get any? When your tummy's rumbling, it's hard to think about anything else! Imagine if you were on a whole school bus of hungry kids and the bus broke down in a hot, dry place for hours and hours. Now you're just beginning to get an idea of how the Israelites felt as they crossed the desert. Let's read about it straight from God's Word.

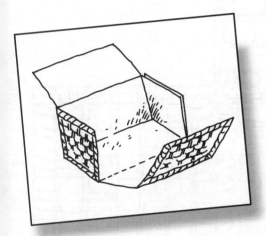

Have volunteers take turns reading Exodus 16:2–3, 11–16, 35; 17:1–6.

- ■ **Do you think God was frustrated with his people? Explain.**

- ■ **If you had to pick one food, and that was the only thing you got to eat for the next five years, what would you choose?**

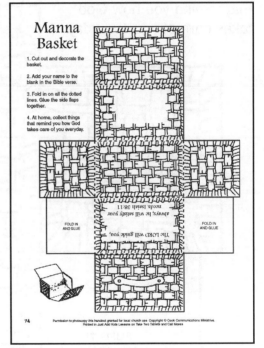

Manna Basket

1. Cut out and decorate the basket.

2. Add your name to the blank in the Bible verse.

3. Fold in on all the dotted lines. Glue the side flaps together.

4. At home, collect things that remind you how God takes care of you everyday.

always, he will satisfy your needs Isaiah 58:11

FOLD IN AND GLUE

FOLD IN AND GLUE

"The LORD will guide you,

74   Permission to photocopy this handout granted for local church use. Copyright © Cook Communications Ministries. Printed in Just Add Kids Lessons on Take Two Tablets and Call Moses.

God's people got to go out every morning and gather manna from the ground. Today we're going to make our own manna baskets. Distribute the "Manna Basket" handouts (p. 74). **Before we put them together, take a minute to put your name right smack in the middle of the Bible verse. Then find a partner and read the verse to each other, filling in your partner's name.** Lead kids through the assembly steps on the handout.

When you take your basket home, drop in little things that remind you of how God takes care of what you need every day. Invite your family to add things too.

- ■ **What might you put in your basket?**

What needs can we pray about today? Let kids share, then pray with them. **Dear God, thank you for inviting us to call you "Daddy." Thank you for moms and dads who look after every day. Thank you for giving them what they need to take care of us. We pray for the needs of (mention kids' concerns). We love you and thank you for keeping us in the palm of your hand, amen.**

Manna Basket

1. Cut out and decorate the basket.

2. Add your name to the blank in the Bible verse.

3. Fold in on all the dotted lines. Glue the side flaps together.

4. At home, collect things that remind you how God takes care of you everyday.

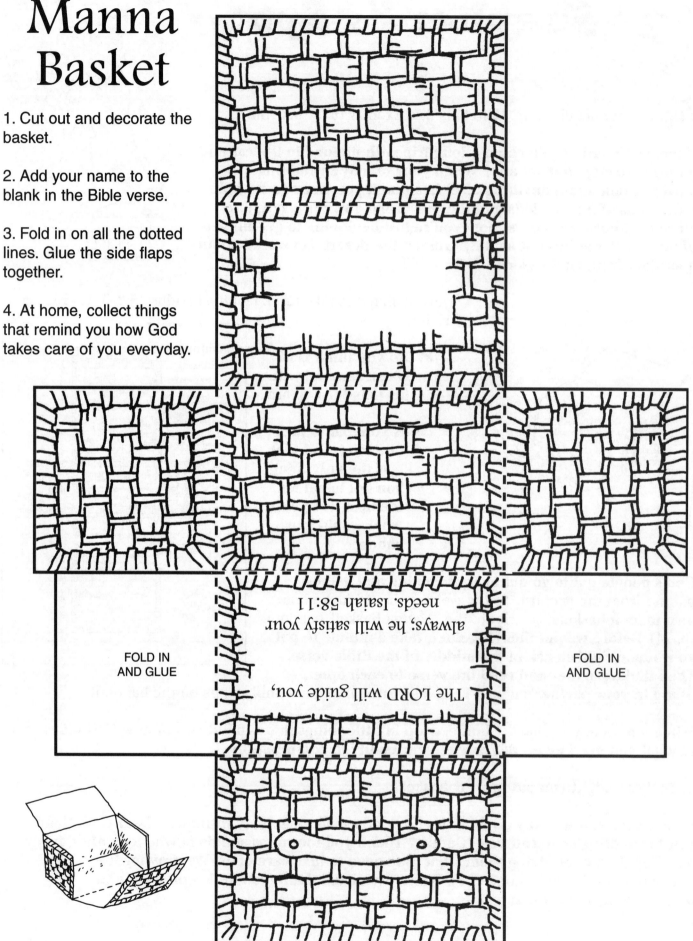

FOLD IN AND GLUE

FOLD IN AND GLUE

The LORD will guide you, always; he will satisfy your needs. Isaiah 58:11

Workshop Wonders

Before class cut the white fun foam into 3-inch squares and the brown foam into 3 1/2-inch squares. Cut a set for each of your kids. You may wish to make a sample of the bread refrigerator magnet for your class to follow.

On class day pass out the scrap paper and pencils. **I'd like each of you to jot down the time of day you feel the hungriest. Is it breakfast? Maybe after soccer practice? Think and write!** Ask volunteers to share their thoughts. **In today's Bible story, the Israelites want to return to Egypt where they had plenty of food to eat. Never mind the slavery and hard work they endured. God's people griped and groaned to Moses anyway. Hunger has a way of making all of us cranky.** Break apart the slices of rye bread and distribute. **No nibbling just yet. God heard his hungry people's call and provided them with food, sweet flakes of manna to erase their tummy aches. Take your piece of rye bread and go ahead and erase the hungry time printed on your paper!**

The sticky gluten in the rye bread will act like an eraser removing the marks from the paper (and from hands too!). When kids have finished erasing, pass out the wet wipes to clean hands and then let them butter clean slices of bread for snacking.

■ **What do you usually eat for breakfast? Where does it come from? What would it be like to gather it from the ground every morning?**

Now let's make a bread magnet to stick to our refrigerators at home to remind us that God provides for our needs each day. Distribute pairs of brown and white foam squares. **Use your scissors to snip the white foam into a bread shape like the one I have here.** Hold up the sample magnet you made before class. Suggest that kids fold the square foam in half and cut out the shape. **Glue the white foam to the brown foam square. Be sure to cut the brown foam into a slightly larger bread shape using the white bread as your guide.**

Trim magnetic strips into 1-inch lengths for each child. Have the children take the paper off the back of the magnetic strip and adhere it to the brown foam. **Now we need to write a reminder on the white bread.** Use pens to write, "God takes care of me." **Just as our magnet will stick to our refrigerators at home, let's remember to stick with God. He promises to take care of our needs.**

Fold down the corners to start your paper airplane.

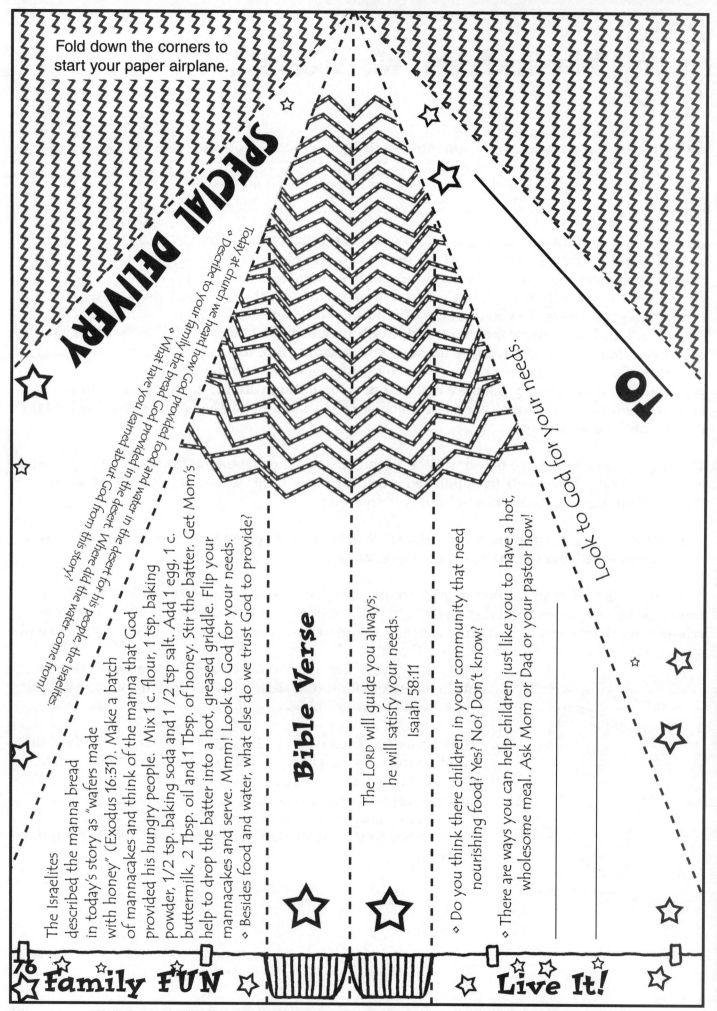

SPECIAL DELIVERY

TO

Look to God for your needs.

The Israelites described the manna bread in today's story as "wafers made with honey" (Exodus 16:31). Make a batch of mannacakes and think of the manna that God provided his hungry people. Mix 1 c. flour, 1 tsp. baking powder, 1/2 tsp. baking soda and 1 1/2 tsp salt. Add 1 egg, 1 c. buttermilk, 2 Tbsp. oil and 1 Tbsp. of honey. Stir the batter. Get Mom's help to drop the batter into a hot, greased griddle. Flip your mannacakes and serve. Mmm! Look to God for your needs.

◊ Besides food and water, what else do we trust God to provide?

Today at church we heard how God provided food and water in the desert. Where did the water come from?

Describe to your family the bread God provided in the desert. What have you learned about God from this story?

Bible Verse

The LORD will guide you always; he will satisfy your needs.
Isaiah 58:11

◊ Do you think there children in your community that need nourishing food? Yes? No? Don't know?

◊ There are ways you can help children just like you to have a hot, wholesome meal. Ask Mom or Dad or your pastor how!

76

Family FUN

Live It!

Welcome Words of Wisdom

Get Set
LARGE GROUP ■ Greet kids and do a puppet skit. Schooner sees the wisdom of a wise mentor for Moses.

❏ large bird puppet ❏ puppeteer

Bible 4U! Instant Drama
LARGE GROUP ■ An amusing narrator observes as father-in-law Jethro pays a visit to an overworked Moses.

❏ actors ❏ copies of the pp. 80–81, Wise Up script ❏ 4 numbered balls ❏ bag
Optional: ❏ robe ❏ fun hats ❏ cane ❏ table and chair ❏ cactus plants

Shepherd's Spot
SMALL GROUP ■ Make an autograph book to collect good advice from godly mentors. Share concerns and pray together. Send home the Special Delivery handout.

❏ Bibles ❏ pencils ❏ scissors ❏ glue sticks ❏ copies of p. 84, Take My Advice
❏ copies of p. 86, Special Delivery

Workshop Wonders
SMALL GROUP ■ Make a simple game board. Then have fun with a bean-bag toss to reinforce today's life application truth.

❏ poster board ❏ yardstick ❏ markers ❏ two bean bags ❏ pencils and paper

Bible Basis Jethro visits Moses Exodus 18:5–9, 13, 17–19, 24–25

Learn It! God gives wise mentors.

Live It! Be open to wise teaching.

Bible Verse Listen to advice and accept instruction, and in the end you will be wise. Proverbs 19:20

Quick Takes

Exodus 18:5–9, 13, 17–19, 24–25

Jethro, Moses' father-in-law, together with Moses' sons and wife, came to him in the desert, where he was camped near the mountain of God.

6 Jethro had sent word to him, "I, your father-in-law Jethro, am coming to you with your wife and her two sons."

7 So Moses went out to meet his father-in-law and bowed down and kissed him. They greeted each other and then went into the tent.

8 Moses told his father-in-law about everything the LORD had done to Pharaoh and the Egyptians for Israel's sake and about all the hardships they had met along the way and how the LORD had saved them.

9 Jethro was delighted to hear about all the good things the LORD had done for Israel in rescuing them from the hand of the Egyptians.

13 The next day Moses took his seat to serve as judge for the people, and they stood round him from morning till evening.

17 Moses' father-in-law replied, "What you are doing is not good.

18 You and these people who come to you will only wear yourselves out. The work is too heavy for you; you cannot handle it alone.

19 Listen now to me and I will give you some advice, and may God be with you. You must be the people's representative before God and bring their disputes to him.

24 Moses listened to his father-in-law and did everything he said.

25 He chose capable men from all Israel and made them leaders of the people, officials over thousands, hundreds, fifties and tens.

Insights

God provided the Israelite food from his own hand. He helped them defeat the attacking Amalekites. Then, with the crises past, the Israelites settled into daily life. Have you ever camped in a crowded campground where you could hear babies wailing, dogs barking, music thrumming and all the details of the squabble going on in the next tent? Multiply that scene to include at least a million and a half people. Make it hot and dry and limit the access to water. Sound fun? In the din of the massive encampment, disputes cropped up like dandelions. As the default judge, Moses handled them all. Enter Jethro. Moses' father-in-law comes to the camp bringing Moses' wife and two sons.

With daylight comes the usual throng of petitioners to Moses' "court." Jethro finds the scene appalling. Why would this history-making man of God try to settle the disputes of such a hoard of people? "What is this you are doing for the people?" Can you just see the wise old man gently chiding his precious son-in-law?

Jethro suggests appointing judges who will hear ordinary cases. The judges can bring difficult cases direct to Moses.

Suppose Moses had responded with pride and self-importance. "Who are you to tell me what to do? Am I not the one God chose to lead his people? Was it not my staff that parted the waters?" Though greater than any leader Israel had ever known, Moses "listened to his father-in-law" and did everything he said. And so Moses' burden was lifted and he went on to talk with God on Mt. Sinai.

In our culture, it feels foreign to accept the counsel of elders. We pride ourselves in being independent thinkers. Moses sets us a golden example. He listened and things got better. Use this lesson to help children see that listening to wise leaders can lead us to a better life and a closer walk with God.

Option Get Set

Welcome, everyone! Now you look like a bunch of smart kids. Do you ever need advice from someone who's older and wiser? Would you believe that even Moses needed advice along the way? I know someone who's always ready to give advice. He has feathers and wings. *Schooner pops up.*

Schooner: That's food for thought, boss.
Leader: What is, Schooner?

Schooner: That Moses would need advice.
Leader: Yes, I think so too.

Schooner: Mighty *Moooooooses.*
Leader: Even Moses, a great Jewish leader and prophet needed a wise mentor.

Schooner: Why, boss?
Leader: A wise mentor gives good advice.

Schooner: Mentor…Mighty…*Moooooooses.*
Leader: And that's just what his father-in-law, Jethro, did in today's Bible story.

Schooner: Mentor…Mighty…*Moooooooses.*
Leader: Jethro gave Moses good advice.

Schooner: *Moooooooses.*
Leader: Ok, Schooner. You're beginning to sound like a parrot.

Schooner: Just figuring that out, boss? *Squawk!*
Leader: Very funny.

Schooner: It is funny. Can we say it together?
Leader: I really don't think we…

Schooner: Pretty please with cheese on top?
Leader: *(rolls eyes and motions to the group)*

Leader and Schooner: *(have the group join in)* Mentor…Mighty…*Moooooooses.*

Leader: I hope you got that out of your system.

Schooner: *(chuckles)* We'll see!
Leader: So Moses listened to Jethro's advice.

Schooner: And what was that, boss?
Leader: Moses was the leader of his people but also a judge.

Schooner: Like the judges on court TV?
Leader: People brought Moses their problems and he decided what to do.

Schooner: I can see a problem already, boss.
Leader: What problem is that, Schooner?

Schooner: Mentors give wise advice, right?
Leader: That's right.

Schooner: Judges give wise advice.

Leader: Correct again.

Schooner: But that's my question.
Leader: I'm sorry, Schooner, I don't follow.

Schooner: What if people don't listen to the wise advice?
Leader: Hmm.

Schooner: People don't like to be told what to do.
Leader: I'd have to say, neither do parrots.

Schooner: *Squawk!* I *usually* listen to you, don't I, boss?
Leader: Sooner or later.

Schooner: You always give me good advice.
Leader: Thank you, Schooner.

Schooner: Yeah, well it could be a while before it happens again.
Leader: *(ignores Schooner)* Moses listened to Jethro's advice and put it into action.

Schooner: An action plan.
Leader: You could say that.

Schooner: Hey, does that make Mighty Moses an action hero?
Leader: Well…no it doesn't. But Moses made a wise choice and because he did he had less work to do as judge.

Schooner: Mentor…Mighty…*Moooooooses*—Action Hero!
Leader: I'm losing control. I can feel it.

Schooner: Mentor…Mighty…*Moooooooses*—Action Hero!
Leader: Schooner, we have so much to do….

Schooner: Do you think he also picked a peck of pickled peppers?
Leader: *(with a sly smile)* No, but he might have picked a peck of pickled *parrots.*

Schooner: Hey, that's not funny!
Leader: Here's one more — Bright…Brilliant…Boss…Bible 4U!

Schooner: I get it. Bible 4U! up next.
Leader: Wise bird.

Bible 4U!

We're in the desert today. It's hot and dry and windy. Thousands of people are crowded around and everyone's crabby. And no one has had a bath in ages! That's the setting for today's Bible 4U! drama. Moses led the Israelites out of Egypt, across the Red Sea and into the desert. When a need popped up, God met it. Now the one with the need was Moses.

Moses' wisdom settled many disputes among God's people. I'd like you to imagine Judge Moses sitting on the bench in his desert courtroom. He hears: "The people rest, your Honor," but he's thinking, "I'm the one that needs the rest!" Thousands of problems multiplied by thousands of hot and tired people.

As we'll hear, Moses tried helping everyone, but he was putting in overtime. Moses needed help, and he got it from his father-in-law, Jethro Let's listen.

Instant Prep
Choose confident readers to play the Narrator, Moses and Jethro. Give each of them a copy of the "Wise Up!" script below.

for Overachievers
Have a three-person drama team prepare the story. Gather a judge's robe for Moses and a comical hat for the narrator. Provide an elderly Jethro a cane and hat. Set up a table and chair for Moses. Cactus plants for a desert environment would be a plus! Begin the drama with a line of "restless" people waiting at Moses' table (including narrator). Jethro waits off stage.

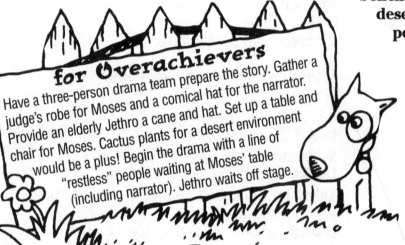

Wise Up!
Based on Exodus 18

Narrator: *(use hand to fan face)* I've waited in this line so long I've grown roots. It's hot. And all these bodies just make it hotter. The crowd keeps pushing me, hoping to get closer to Moses. *(Shakes head)* How Moses sits there, from morning till night…

Moses: *(leans back in chair)* Oi, I'm tired! I need a break.

Narrator: Hmm. I wonder who Moses turns to for advice. *(Holds up hand over eyes to look in the distance)* Someone's coming.

Jethro shuffles in with his cane. Bent over, he takes short, exacting steps.

Moses: Lo and behold! It's my father-in-law, Jethro.

Narrator: As was custom, Moses greets Jethro with a kiss.

Moses: *(freezes in place)* A kiss?

Narrator: Yes. It says right here in the script, "As was custom, Moses greets Jethro with a kiss."

Moses: How about I just give him a high-five instead?

Narrator: *(Shrugs shoulders)* I suppose. *(Clears throat)* As was custom Moses greets Jethro with a high-five. *(Moses and Jethro high-five.)*

Jethro: *(in a shaky, ancient voice)* Moses, my son. It is good to see you! My you've grown.

Moses: You think so? The wife has me on that all-protein diet. And I lift weights after work.

Jethro looks around to see all the people waiting for Judge Moses.

Jethro: From the looks of it, it's the weight of the world, my son. You look busy.

Moses: *(sighs)* Very.

Narrator: *(sighs)* Very.

Moses: The docket's full almost everyday, Pops. But I want to help our people. God has chosen me leader.

Narrator: Moses is a good leader.

Jethro: *(points cane at the Narrator)* My Moses is a *great* leader. But enough is enough. It's time for a little advice. Moses, step into my chat room.

Jethro and Moses walk off a bit and talk.

Narrator: Moses and Jethro talk for a long time. The people waiting for help throw up their hands and go home. *(Kids waiting in line throw up their hands and go sit down.)* And still the two men talk.

Moses: *(talks for a bit longer)* So that's all of it since I last saw you.

Jethro: *(let's out a deep breath)* My, my. Sounds like God has been doing some mighty good things! But I already see the problem.

Narrator: I see the problem too.

Moses: What problem?

Jethro: You're doing too much!

Narrator: I tried telling him that... "You're doing too much!"

Moses: *(turns to the Narrator)* No you didn't.

Narrator: Well, I thought about it.

Moses: Thought about, doesn't count.

Jethro: May I continue?

Narrator and Moses: Of course.

Jethro: Wise up, Moses. You need help. With all these people come many problems. You're only one man—with only two ears. Did you really think you could do all this yourself?

Moses: *(shrugs shoulders and looks at floor.)*

Narrator: I think that means yes.

Moses: *(smirks at the Narrator)* Just what would we do without you?

Narrator: *(lifts chin in the air and ignores Moses)* The conversation changes. This time Jethro does the talking and Moses listens.

Moses: I'm listening, Jethro. Your wise advice means a lot to me.

Jethro and Moses huddle and talk some more.

Narrator: As twilight fades and darkness settles, Moses now knows what he needs to do.

Moses: I now know what I need to do!

Narrator: Moses is excited!

Moses: I must appoint leaders from within the people. They can help judge some of these weighty matters. I will set leaders over thousands of people and then hundreds of people and finally groups of fifties and tens.

Jethro: *(slaps his knee)* You go, Moses!

Narrator: *(looks respectfully at Jethro)* A chip off the old block, I'd say.

Moses: And best of all God's people will go home satisfied. And I can get some rest! Thank you, Pops.

Jethro tips his hat and exits.

Narrator: Moses learned that he didn't have to have all the answers. Getting help is a wise thing. That's why God gives us wise teachers and mentors.

Moses: So let's remember to be open to wise teaching.

Narrator: *(smiles broadly)* You took the words right out of my mouth, Moses.

Moses: I'm not surprised!

Sometimes even the wise need an advisor. Let's see how wise you were in sorting out the highlights in today's story.

Toss the four numbered balls to different parts of the room. Bring the kids with the balls to the front one-by-one and ask these questions. Allow kids to get help from the group if they need it. After each correct answer, let kids drop the ball into a bag.

 ■ **What were all the roles Moses played as the leader of the nation of Israel?**

 ■ **Since battles were past, what did Moses do every day?**

 ■ **What advice did Jethro give Moses?**

 ■ **Who gives you good advice?**

Moses was a man of God, a wise leader, and a really smart guy! But he was so busy fixing everything for the nation of Israel that he couldn't see how much he needed to fix a few things for himself. That's where Jethro came into the picture. There's an old expression that says, "I can't see the forest for the trees." In other words, Moses was so caught up in settling arguments and disputes that he couldn't step back and say, "Hey! Other people could help me with this. If I'm going to be a good leader, I need to get some rest."

Bible Verse
Listen to advice and accept instruction, and in the end you will be wise.
Proverbs 19:20

But Jethro saw that right away. And Jethro gave advice the way we all like to get it. He took time to listen to Moses and together they praised God for helping Israel. Then he watched what went on. He saw how much Moses was trying to do all by himself. He spoke kindly to Moses, and Moses was glad to hear what he had to say.

I'm sure you have all had some great "Jethros" in your life—godly people who care about you and want to help you on your way. Today in your shepherd groups you'll learn a fun way to get even more good advice from them than ever!

Dismiss kids to their shepherd groups.

Gather your small group and help kids find Exodus 18 in their Bibles.

You know what's amazing about this week's story? Nothing terrible happened! No hailstorms, frog invasions or clattering armies in pursuit. Not one big disaster. Just little disasters—lots of them. And they all ended up in Moses' lap. Let's read about it straight from God's Word. Ask volunteers to read these passages aloud: Exodus 18:5–9, 13, 17–19, 24–25.

■ **What do you think some of the squabbles might have been about?**

Jethro arrived at the Israelite camp, bringing the rest of Moses' family. Jethro was Moses' father-in-law. You can tell these two men loved each other very much.

■ **What was the advice Jethro had for Moses?**

Moses was a great and wise man of God. God used him to do miracles no one else had ever done. But when his father-in-law offered advice, he listened. Jethro shared God's wisdom and brought peace to Moses' busy life. God brings people like that into our lives today, people who help us see what's best and how to use our time. The booklet we're going to make today will help you find some of those people who are important to you. Let them autograph your book and offer you some gems of wisdom!

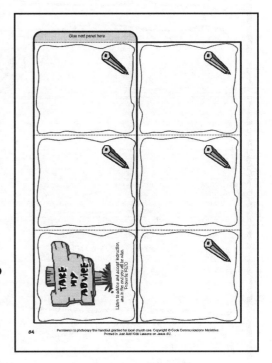

Distribute the "Take My Advice" handouts (p. 84). Have kids cut out the two sections of three boxes each. Make one long strip by gluing the tab at the end of the first section to the back of the second section. Then accordion-fold the pages to form a book. Encourage kids to tell whose advice they'll seek.

As we pray today, let's thank God for the wise people he's brought into our lives. I'll pause in the middle of my prayer, and you can say the names of people you're thinking of. Bow heads in prayer. **Dear heavenly Father, thank you for sending special people into our lives who guide us and point the way to you. We thank you especially for** (let kids list people). **Bless these people, we pray. In Jesus name, amen.**

Glue next panel here

Listen to advice and accept instruction, and in the end you will be wise.
Proverbs 19:20

TAKE MY ADVICE

Workshop Wonders

Make simple beanbags using rice-filled balloons or fill a child's size sock, glove or mitten with dried beans. Be sure to tie or knot the end.

Answers, answers! **As we heard in today's Bible story a lot of people needed Moses' help. What's a leader to do? Fortunately, Moses had someone in his life that cared—his father-in-law Jethro. Jethro was a wise mentor.**

■ **Other than your family, who would you go to for help or advice?**

Jethro instructed Moses that the work he had taken on was too much for him. As top judge, Moses was wearing himself out. Moses listened to the wise advice of Jethro and "chose capable men from all Israel and made them leaders of the people, officials over thousands, hundreds, fifties and tens." (Exodus 18:25) Good advice!

■ **Have you ever given good advice to someone? What did you say?**

Let's play a game that will help us practice listening to wise mentors.

Hand a marker and the yardstick to a volunteer and make a tic-tac-toe grid on the poster board. When finished, call on other volunteers to color in the squares and print in the following "point" amounts: 1,000, 100, 50 or 10—he numbers mentioned in Exodus 25. Print today's Bible verse in the middle square as well. Place the game board in the middle of the room and ask kids to pair up.

Being open to wise teaching takes two! Hand the first pair of players the beanbags. Have kids decide who will be the Wise Mentor and who the Great Listener for this round of play. **I will read a situation out loud. Wise Mentors, help your partner come up with a solution to the problem. Then share it with the group. The group will offer its advice as well. When finished, both players on the team will toss their beanbags at the game board. You want the two beanbags to touch in order for the you and your teammate to collect the points. Like Moses, I'll be the judge if conflicts arise.** Appoint a volunteer to keep a running tally on the board or on a sheet of paper. Have players stand 10 feet back from the board to start play.

Suggested situations:
- A friend is down because he's moving out of state. What advice can you give?
- A new kid at school sits all alone at lunch. What advice can you give him or her?
- Your best friend wants to take a candy bar without paying the clerk. Your advice?
- A teammate is unhappy because her mistake allowed the winning goal to score. Your advice?
- You and your brother or sister fight constantly. Who can you go to for helpful advice?
- There's a kid at school who always picks on you and makes fun of you in front of your classmates. Who can give you wise advice?

Add situations as time allows. Don't forget to add up the points! **God sends us wise mentors. Let's always be open to wise teaching.**

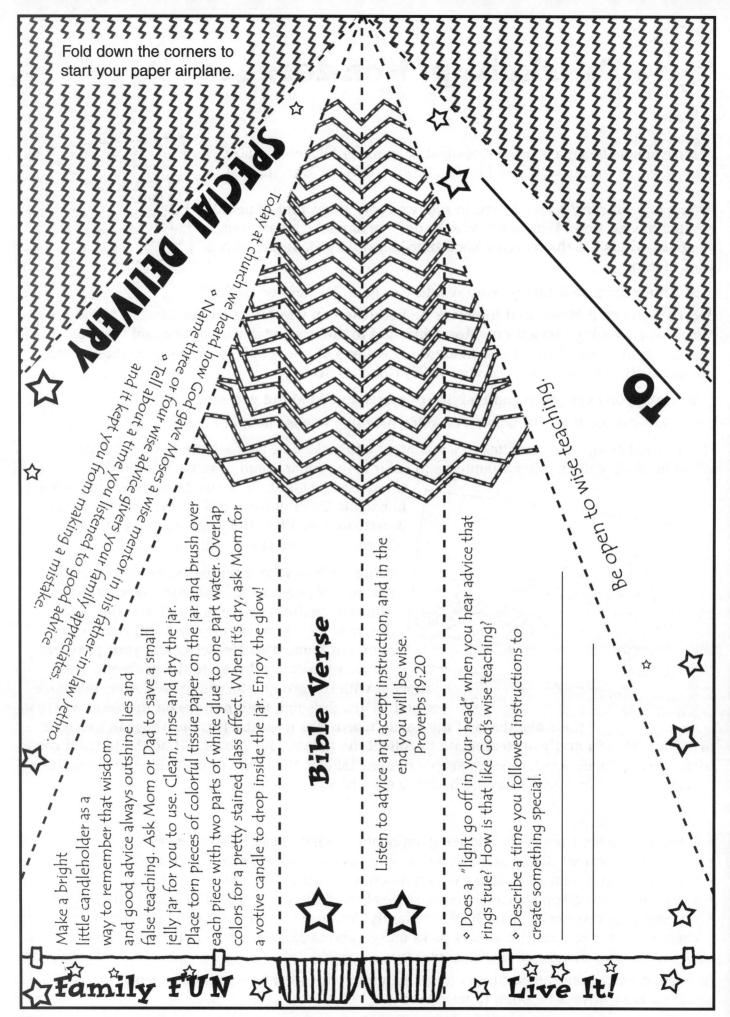

Fold down the corners to start your paper airplane.

SPECIAL DELIVERY

TO

Be open to wise teaching.

Today at church we heard how God gave Moses a wise mentor in his father-in-law Jethro.

◊ Name three or four wise advice givers and it kept you from making a mistake.

◊ Tell about a time you listened to good advice and how your family appreciates.

Make a bright little candleholder as a way to remember that wisdom and good advice always outshine lies and false teaching. Ask Mom or Dad to save a small jelly jar for you to use. Clean, rinse and dry the jar. Place torn pieces of colorful tissue paper on the jar and brush over each piece with two parts of white glue to one part water. Overlap colors for a pretty stained glass effect. When it's dry, ask Mom for a votive candle to drop inside the jar. Enjoy the glow!

Bible Verse

Listen to advice and accept instruction, and in the end you will be wise.
Proverbs 19:20

◊ Does a "light go off in your head" when you hear advice that rings true? How is that like God's wise teaching?

◊ Describe a time you followed instructions to create something special.

Family FUN

Live It!

With God's Heart

Get Set

LARGE GROUP ■ Greet kids and do a puppet skit. Schooner learns that God wants to be #1 in our lives.

❏ large bird puppet ❏ puppeteer

Bible 4U! Instant Drama

LARGE GROUP ■ Elihu and Adina, brother and sister duo, find an ancient journal that reveals an eyewitness's experience at the foot of Mt. Sinai.

❏ actors ❏ copies of pp. 90–91, Write On script ❏ 4 numbered balls ❏ bag
Optional: ❏ antiqued journal ❏ Bibletime costumes

Shepherd's Spot

SMALL GROUP ■ Build simple stair steps with the first four commandments. Share concerns and pray together. Send home the Special Delivery handout.

❏ Bibles ❏ pencils ❏ scissors ❏ glue sticks ❏ copies of p. 94, Steps to Obedience, Part 1 ❏ copies of p. 96, Special Delivery Optional: ❏ construction paper

Workshop Wonders

SMALL GROUP ■ Have your kids follow the rules of science to discover candy that commands Bible verse attention.

❏ tablecloth ❏ Bibles ❏ Smarties® candies ❏ coffee filter ❏ bowl of water
❏ paper plates ❏ drinking glass ❏ dark corn syrup ❏ cooking oil ❏ measuring cups Optional: ❏ grape ❏ penny

Bible Basis
Ten Commandments
Part 1
Exodus 19:1–2, 16–19; 20:1–11

Learn It!
God wants us to know him.

Live It!
Love and honor God.

Bible Verse
Love the Lord your God with all your heart and with all your soul and with all your mind." This is the first and greatest commandment. Matthew 22:37–38.

Quick Takes

In the third month after the Israelites left Egypt—on the very day—they came to the Desert of Sinai.

2 After they set out from Rephidim, they entered the Desert of Sinai, and Israel camped there in the desert in front of the mountain.

16 On the morning of the third day there was thunder and lightning, with a thick cloud over the mountain, and a very loud trumpet blast. Everyone in the camp trembled.

17 Then Moses led the people out of the camp to meet with God, and they stood at the foot of the mountain.

18 Mount Sinai was covered with smoke, because the Lord descended on it in fire. The smoke billowed up from it like smoke from a furnace, the whole mountain trembled violently,

19 and the sound of the trumpet grew louder and louder. Then Moses spoke and the voice of God answered him.

20:1 And God spoke all these words:

2 "I am the Lord your God, who brought you out of Egypt, out of the land of slavery.

3 "You shall have no other gods before me.

4 "You shall not make for yourself an idol in the form of anything in heaven above or on the earth beneath or in the waters below.

5 You shall not bow down to them or worship them; for I, the Lord your God, am a jealous God, punishing the children for the sin of the fathers to the third and fourth generation of those who hate me,

6 but showing love to a thousand generations of those who love me and keep my commandments.

7 "You shall not misuse the name of the Lord your God, for the Lord will not hold anyone guiltless who misuses his name.

8 "Remember the Sabbath day by keeping it holy.

9 Six days you shall labor and do all your work,

10 but the seventh day is a Sabbath to the Lord your God. On it you shall not do any work, neither you, nor your son or daughter, nor your manservant or maidservant, nor your animals, nor the alien within your gates.

11 For in six days the Lord made the heavens and the earth, the sea, and all that is in them, but he rested on the seventh day. Therefore the Lord blessed the Sabbath day and made it holy.

Insights

After three months of traveling, the Israelites made camp in front of Mount Sinai. "Then Moses went up to God" (Exodus 19:3). That's certainly not the way we're accustomed to communicating with our Creator! God allowed Moses unique contact with him to shape the Israelites into his own treasured possession.

If you've never done it before, pause to read Exodus 19 and 20 together. They are two sides of the same window into the heart of God. God paints for Moses an amazing word picture of his care of the people of Israel. "This is what you are to say to the house of Jacob and what you are to tell the people of Israel: 'You yourselves have seen what I did to Egypt, and how I carried you on eagles' wings and brought you to myself.'"

God called his people into a lasting relationship with him. By living by these laws, the Israelites would covenant with God and serve as a light to the world. He called them into the desert for this very purpose and gave Moses words of life to take with him down the mountain.

God emphasizes being "one" because the Jews had spent four hundred years in Egypt's culture of many gods. Many of the key gods of Egypt were represented by animals, such as cows, cats, falcons and bulls. Egyptians were deeply involved in magic. Priests were seldom seen by common people—they secreted themselves away in temples preparing magic potions. God sets himself apart from these idols of wood and stone.

God longed for a response of loving obedience from these people on whom he'd showed so much care. God wants us to cherish him as he cherishes us. Use this lesson to show kids how God's tender father-heart longs for their loving respect and obedience.

Option · Get Set

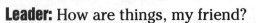

Welcome all! Of all the things mentioned in the Bible, the Ten Commandments would make anyone's Top 10 list. And good thing! God wants us to know, love and honor him above all else—and his commandments tell us how to do just that. Schooner, come and join me. *Schooner pops up.*

Leader: How are things, my friend?

Schooner: G-r-r-r-reat.

Leader: Anything to share with us today?

Schooner: Let see. *(Suddenly brightens)* My soccer team made the playoffs.

Leader: Congratulations! I didn't know you played soccer, Schooner.

Schooner: Kinda.

Leader: What do you mean? Do you or don't you play soccer?

Schooner: Well…we use a sock.

Leader: *(scratches head)* There's no sock in soccer, Schooner.

Schooner: The players wear socks.

Leader: Sure, but…

Schooner: …very colorful ones, too. Purple, red, green…polka dotted.

Leader: Polka dots?

Schooner: *(whispers)* My favorite!

Leader: But socks have nothing to do with the game of soccer, Schooner.

Schooner: Maybe not the way *you* play it.

Leader: *(sighs)* You win, Schooner. Tell us your team's name.

Schooner: The Mighty Clucks.

Leader: Sounds like a bunch of chickens.

Schooner: Drumsticks make good kickers.

Leader: The Mighty Clucks are in the playoffs.

Schooner: Yup.

Leader: That's wonderful.

Schooner: Wonderful only if we win, boss.

Leader: That would make the team happy?

Schooner: Sure. Being on top…winning…being #1….now that's the life.

Leader: Many people would agree with you, Schooner.

Schooner: *(clears throat)* Team cheer! *We're #1, under the Sun! We're #1, second to none! Squawk!*

Leader: What if it rains on game day?

Schooner: No sun? Hadn't thought of that.

Leader: While you think, Schooner, I'll talk about God's Ten Commandments.

Schooner: Today's Bible story.

Leader: Yes. The Ten Commandments are God's rules to live by.

Schooner: So tell us the #1 commandment.

Leader: God is #1, Schooner. We are to worship the one true God.

Schooner: *God's #1, second to none!*

Leader: And the second commandment tells us not to worship statues.

Schooner: That's silly, boss.

Leader: In Bible times, the Egyptians worshiped many idols or statues. Let's see…there's was Ra the god of the sun, Shu, the god of the air and the god of rain was…

Schooner: Rain. That reminds me.

Leader: Yes?

Schooner: I have to come up with a new team cheer before it rains!

Leader: Let's stick with God's commandments for now, shall we?

Schooner: I'm listening, boss.

Leader: We're supposed to speak God's name with respect.

Schooner: Of course. He's God!

Leader: And finally, set aside a special day to worship God.

Schooner: *(nods head to count up)* That's not ten. Didn't you say there are Ten Commandments, boss?

Leader: Yes. But I think that's enough for today, Schooner.

Schooner: I got it!

Leader: What?

Schooner: A cheer! How's this? *We're #1—come rain or come sun!*

Leader: *(sighs)* You're a little distracted today, Schooner. Ahead to Bible 4U!

Bible 4U!

It's somewhere around the year 1211 BC in the land of Canaan. A brother and sister make a remarkable discovery! At the bottom of an empty jar they find a journal written years before by a young boy named Amariah. Amazingly, Amariah was camping with his family at the base of Mt. Sinai when the mountain blew its top! That was the day God gave Moses the Ten Commandments cut into stone tablets.

Lightning and thunder rocked Mt. Sinai. A mountain trembling in smoke and fire! Hear the trumpet blasts, louder and louder, as they split the air in two.

Amariah was so inspired by what he saw and heard that he wrote it all down on an animal skin scroll—Bibletime paper. I'm sure his hand shook with fright as he recorded his thoughts.

Today, we can find God's laws written on the pages of the Bible. But God wants them written on our hearts too. By honoring God's Word, we honor God himself. Let's give a listen to what happens when Elihu and his sister Adina meet a much older stranger named Amariah.

Write On
Based on Exodus 19-20

Elihu: (excitedly) The villagers are all talking!

Adina: You said it, brother. An eyewitness account of the giving of the law.

Elihu: (shakes head in disbelief) From God's mouth to the prophet Moses' ears. It's unbelievable.

Adina: (reaches into the clay pot and picks up the journal.) Believe it. I have the diary right here in my hand. It's not every day we find a hundred-year-old journal.

Elihu: Correction, sister. I found it.

Adina: Correction, brother. I found it.

Elihu: But I got to it first.

Adina: And you almost tore the cover.

Elihu: Almost doesn't count.

Adina: (folds arms and turns away) You're impossible.

Elihu: Can we get back to the journal?

Adina: (relents) A Ten Commandment experience with such sparkle and sizzle must stay with you forever—even if you live to be a hundred!

Elihu: Open the journal and read the beginning again.

Adina: Which part? Where Mt. Sinai rocks and rolls or when Moses speaks and God answers?

Elihu: That's it!

Adina: (opens the journal and begins to read) "And God spoke all these words: I am the

Lord your God, who brought you out of Egypt, out of the land of slavery. *(Adina is interrupted by a stranger who enters from offstage.)*

Amariah: Excuse me. I heard talk in the village of a journal found by a brother and sister. Would that be you two?

Elihu: *(suspiciously)* What's it to you?

Adina: Don't be rude, brother. Yes, we found a journal.

Amariah: Can I see it?

Elihu: Why?

Amariah: It may be mine.

Elihu: Not so fast. If it's really yours, tell us where we found it.

Amariah: In a small cave behind the old well in the hills of Shiloh. I placed it in a large clay pot.

Wide-eyed, Adina and Elihu look at each other.

Adina: *(whispers to Elihu)* I think it's him.

Elihu: Not so fast. *(Takes the journal from Adina and flips through it.)* Tell us more.

Amariah: If you look at the journal's inside cover you'll see the name, "Amariah" printed, as a child would write.

Adina and Elihu search the inside cover.

Amariah: *(looks off as if remembering and continues)* I was a very young boy the day God came to Mt. Sinai. I remember Moses, our leader, had us change into clean clothes.

Adina: *(thinks a bit)* When someone special comes to our house Mama makes us get dressed up.

Amariah: Moses told us that the Lord wanted his people to know him and to remember that his power alone delivered us from Egypt's Pharaoh.

Elihu: *(excitedly)* What happened next?

Amariah: We couldn't come too close to the mountain or even touch it. That was God's order.

Elihu: Really?

Amariah: Anyone who touched the mountain would die. We could only approach the mountain when we heard a trumpet blast. *(Shudders at the thought.)* When the trumpet blew it was so loud it frightened me. The midday sky was as dark as night, lightning flashed and the rumbling thunder sounded like a thousand drums. I covered my ears and still I heard it. Everyone was afraid. The ground and the mountain started shaking. An earthquake, I was sure. Then the trumpet sound came again. This time even louder than the first.

Adina: WOW! What happened next?

Elihu: *(reads the journal intently)* Don't interrupt. Let the man talk.

Amariah: Smoke billowed from the mountain and God came down and rested on top of it.

Adina: What did that look like?

Amariah: We saw fiery flames at the top of the mountain. My family stood there amazed. Moses went up the mountain and disappeared into the smoke and clouds.

Elihu: *(reads from the journal)* "When Moses finally came down from the mountain he had two stone tablets—the Ten Commandments that the Lord had given him."

The three actors stand in silence for a few seconds taking in all they've heard.

Elihu: *(Hands the journal to Amariah.)* Sir, I believe this is yours.

Amariah: Thank you. The Ten Commandments have become for all Israelites a way of life. We are special to God, a nation different from all others. That means we are set apart. We are holy.

Adina: We know the laws. Papa taught them to us. He wrote them on our doorway at home. The first four are: Put God First, No Idols, Respect God's Name and Remember God's Day of Rest.

Amariah: Our holy God wants us to be loyal, faithful, obedient and grateful. And I've spent my life trying to do just that.

The three actors walk offstage happy to be in each other's company.

Bible 4U!

Never a dull moment for the Israelites! Today we hear of a camping experience not soon to be forgotten. But as terrifying as it must have been for God's people to witness the sounds and power of his might, God's instructions would serve to educate his people about who he was—the one, the only God—as well as rules on how they were to treat others. As for the Israelites who witnessed the awesome event, God certainly delivered it in style. Lives trembled and quaked but would forever be changed. And that, after all, was the point! Ready for the great ball toss? Grab one if it comes your way.

Toss the four numbered balls to different parts of the room. Bring the kids with the balls to the front one-by-one and ask these questions. Allow kids to get help from the group if they need it. After each correct answer, let kids drop the ball into a bag.

■ Why was the journal Adina and Elihu found in the clay pot such a valuable find?

■ There was a musical instrument talked about in today's drama that many high school bands still use today. Who remembers what that was? (A trumpet.)

■ The weather took a twist the day Moses met God! What weather elements can you remember from today's drama?

■ Tell me the first four of God's Ten Commandments.

God pulled out all the fireworks for his Mt. Sinai appearance. It was a day filled with his power and presence—a day his people would never forget.

And love was at the center of it all. The commandments would help God's beloved people that day to know, love and honor him—even if the experience was a bit frightening! But God's rules were also meant to be passed down to children for generations to come so that they might do the same. No one knew this better than Moses. Once again he spoke to God on a mountaintop and lived to tell about it. Not too many people, past or present, can say that!

Dismiss kids to their shepherd groups.

Bible Verse
Love the Lord your God with all your heart and with all your all soul and with all your mind." This is the first and greatest commandment. Matthew: 22:37–38

② Shepherd's Spot

Gather kids in your small group and help them find Exodus 19 in their Bibles.

Finally the Israelites camped at the base of Mt. Sinai, the holy mountain where God would talk to Moses face to face. How exciting was that! The people had strict orders not to set foot on the mountain. God came down and Moses went up. What do you think the people heard and saw? Have a volunteer read Exodus 19:16–18.

■ **If you were waiting at the bottom of the mountain and saw this happening, what would you say to your neighbor?**

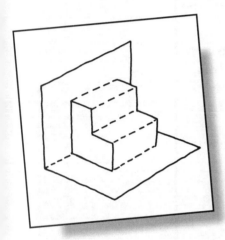

You may remember that the Israelites spent hundreds of years as slaves in Egypt. The Egyptians worshiped all kinds of fake gods made of wood and stone. In the first commandments God gave, he told the people that he was different. He told them how to treat him. Let's see what God said. Have a volunteer read Exodus 20:1–3.

AND GOD SPOKE ALL THESE WORDS:

I am the LORD your God, who brought you out of Egypt, out of the land of slavery. You shall have no other gods before me.

You shall not make for yourself an idol in the form of anything in heaven above or on the earth beneath, or in the waters below. You shall not bow down to them or worship them.

You shall not misuse the name of the LORD your God, for the LORD will not hold anyone guiltless who misuses his name.

Remember the Sabbath day by keeping it holy. Six days you shall labour and do all your work, but the seventh day is a Sabbath to the LORD your God.

◆ STEPS TO OBEDIENCE ◆
PART I, FROM EXODUS 20:1–11

PREPARED BY _____

94   Permission to photocopy this handout granted for local church use. Copyright © Cook Communications Ministries. Printed in Just Add Kids Lessons on Jesus 4U.

     Following these commandments would make the Israelites God's special people. He wanted them to love him every bit as much as he loved them. God wants that same kind of love and obedience from us. Let's make "Steps to Obedience" to remember these first four commandments.

Distribute the "Steps to Obedience" handout, p. 94. Have kids fold it in half on the dotted line and cut the dark lines between the dots. Lay the paper flat again, then valley fold on the middle line and mountain fold on the two dashed lines. Pull the steps forward. If you wish, let kids add a backing sheet of construction paper. Let volunteers read the commandments from the handout again.

■ **What is important to God?**

Let's close with prayer by telling God just how much we love him. I'll start, then wait and let each of you add to the prayer. Begin your prayer. **God, I love you. You're the most important thing in my life.** Pause as kids add their prayers. **Thank you for giving us your Word so we may know you better. Fill us up with love. This we pray, amen.**

AND GOD SPOKE ALL THESE WORDS:

I am the LORD your God, who brought you
out of Egypt, out of the land of slavery.
You shall have no other gods before me.

You shall not make for yourself an idol
in the form of anything in heaven above
or on the earth beneath, or in the waters below.
You shall not bow down to them
or worship them.

You shall not misuse the name of the LORD
your God, for the LORD will not hold anyone
guiltless who misuses his name.

Remember the Sabbath day by keeping it holy.
Six days you shall labor and do all your work,
but the seventh day is a Sabbath
to the LORD your God.

STEPS TO OBEDIENCE
PART 1, FROM EXODUS 20:1-11

PREPARED BY _____

Workshop Wonders

z Before class, cover your activity table. Place the plates, candy, coffee filters and bowl of water at one end of the table. On the opposite end, place the drinking glass, oil, corn syrup and measuring cups. Start your teaching with the candy.

Get List:
- ❑ tablecloth
- ❑ Bibles
- ❑ Smarties® candies
- ❑ coffee filters
- ❑ bowl of water
- ❑ paper plates
- ❑ drinking glass
- ❑ dark corn syrup
- ❑ cooking oil
- ❑ measuring cups

Optional:
- ❑ grape
- ❑ penny

The Israelites had come from the land of Egypt. It was the land of many gods. And to the Egyptians the more gods to worship the better. The God of Israel, however, wanted none of this. He is the only true God and he wanted his people to remember that always.

With Moses as leader, God led his people from Egyptian slavery to the wilderness of the Sinai Desert. Here they camped at the foot of a mountain called Mount Sinai. With thunder and lightning and trumpet blasts God made his presence known with the Ten Commandments.

■ **With God so near, the Israelites trembled with fear. Suppose that happened today. What would the headlines say?**

■ **Open your Bible and read the first four commandments, Exodus 20:1–11. Turn to a partner and tell him or her what they say to you using your own words.**

God's people needed to obey his commandments. But in the days to come that would prove easier said than done for the Israelites. Let's do an experiment that melts "hard hearts" into ones eager to obey and honor God.

Distribute plates, filters and candy, one per student. Set the single piece of candy in the middle of the filter. Have kids dip fingers into the bowl of water and drip five or six drops onto the candies until each is soaked and a small water ring forms on the filter. Wait five minutes. (While you wait, walk to the other end of the table.)

Today's Bible Verse also talks about hearts.

"Love your God with all your heart…Ask a volunteer to pour one-third cup of corn syrup into the empty drinking glass.
And with all your soul…Add one-third cup of cooking oil (slowly down the inside of the glass.)
And with all your mind. Finally, pour in one-third cup of water down the inside of the glass.
"This is the first and greatest commandment." (Matthew 22:37–38)

Allow the contents to settle. **Our Bible verse speaks of three different things: a heart, a soul and a mind.** Have the class observe the now three separate layers of liquid in the glass. **Think of the three separate layers as the heart, soul and mind that make up just one thing—you! May our hearts, souls and minds seek to honor and love God above all else all the days of our lives.** If you wish, have kids drop a candy, a grape, and a penny into the glass and watch as each settles into a different (density) layer.

Back to the candy! Walk back to the other end of the table. Observe how the shell of the round candy has softened and rings of color now decorate the coffee filters. Distribute any extra candies you may have for snacking.

Fold down the corners to start your paper airplane.

SPECIAL DELIVERY

TO

Love and honor God.

Today at church we learned to honor God with the first four commandments. Ask everyone in your school obeyed God's commandments from memory. "If everyone in your family obeyed the Ten Commandments, how might your day change for the better?"

God chose the Israelites to be his special nation. In return he asked for their obedience. Amid thunder and lightning flashes God gave them the Ten Commandments. Find a room at home with a mirror. Turn off the lights and close the blinds. Open a roll of Wintergreen Lifesavers® and pop one into your mouth. Then chew and smile and look into the mirror all at the same time! Watch the mini-lightning flashes as your teeth crush the candy. Love and honor God with the Ten Commandments.

Bible Verse

"Love the Lord your God with all your heart and with all your all soul and with all your mind." This is the first and greatest commandment. Matthew: 22:37–38

◊ What do you think God's people thought the first time they heard the Ten Commandments? What about you?

◊ How can you see God's love for his people in the commandments?

☆ Family FUN ☆

Live It!

The Royal Law

Option — Get Set
LARGE GROUP ■ Greet kids and do a puppet skit. Schooner learns that God's rules of love touch hearts and help all of us get along.

❑ large bird puppet ❑ puppeteer

1 — Bible 4U! Instant Drama
LARGE GROUP ■ With the help of an older man, an Israelite brother and sister learn how God's commandments help us love each other.

❑ 3 actors ❑ copies of pp. 100–101, Scenes from Sinai script ❑ 4 numbered balls ❑ bag

2 — Shepherd's Spot
SMALL GROUP ■ Make a set of stair steps with the last six of the Ten Commandments. Share concerns and pray together. Send home the Special Delivery handout.

❑ Bibles ❑ pencils ❑ scissors ❑ glue sticks ❑ copies of p. 104, Steps to Obedience, Part 2 ❑ copies of p. 106, Special Delivery

Option — Workshop Wonders
SMALL GROUP ■ Review today's love thy neighbor commandments with a tablet snack.

❑ Bibles ❑ graham crackers ❑ vanilla frosting ❑ fruit leather ❑ kitchen shears ❑ drinking straws ❑ fruit ring cereal ❑ decorator gel tubes ❑ plates, napkins, plastic knives

Bible Basis Ten Commandments Part 2 Exodus 20:12–21; 31:18

Learn It! God's rules help us get along.

Live It! Treat people with love and respect.

Bible Verse If you really keep the royal law found in Scripture, "Love your neighbor as yourself," you are doing right. James 2:8

"Honor your father and your mother, so that you may live long in the land the Lord your God is giving you.

13 "You shall not murder.

14 "You shall not commit adultery.

15 "You shall not steal.

16 "You shall not give false testimony against your neighbor.

17 "You shall not covet your neighbor's house. You shall not covet your neighbor's wife, or his manservant or maidservant, his ox or donkey, or anything that belongs to your neighbor."

18 When the people saw the thunder and lightning and heard the trumpet and saw the mountain in smoke, they trembled with fear. They stayed at a distance

19 and said to Moses, "Speak to us yourself and we will listen. But do not have God speak to us or we will die."

20 Moses said to the people, "Do not be afraid. God has come to test you, so that the fear of God will be with you to keep you from sinning."

21 The people remained at a distance, while Moses approached the thick darkness where God was.

31:18 When the Lord finished speaking to Moses on Mount Sinai, he gave him the two tablets of the Testimony, the tablets of stone inscribed by the finger of God.

Insights

Even after all the miracles God did on their behalf, the Israelites were fickle in their allegiance and slow to trust him. So, with the first four commandments, God sets himself apart from the idols of Egypt and asks for the Israelite's unwavering love and obedience. In the remaining commandments, God turns the focus to relationships with people.

Jewish people call this text ten "statements" or "words." Even more than commandments, they are categories, which broadly cover many specifics of Jewish law. Devout Jews study, memorize and cherish these laws, figuratively writing them on their hearts. We Christians find the very nature of the heart of God in the patterns of behavior he lays down for his people.

We learn from this foundational passage that God expects our relationship with him to play out in our relationships with other people. God loved his people both as a community of faith and as individuals. In our culture, we think primarily of individuals. Mideastern culture sees from another perspective. It is a precious privilege to be part of the community of faith. By honoring God's people, they honor the God who loves them.

The Ten Commandments are so fundamental to our thinking we can't even begin to imagine life without them. Our ethics, our legal system and our beliefs about fairness and justice all find their source in the words Moses brought down the mountain from God.

Jews of Jesus time felt his message and his actions undermined the commandments. But he said otherwise. "Do not think that I have come to abolish the Law or the Prophets; I have not come to abolish them but to fulfill them" (Matthew 5:17). Jesus taught us how to live the spirit of the law, holding us to an even higher standard. Use this lesson to help kids see that what we believe about right and wrong is firmly rooted in these commandments, and that God wants us to obey out of love for him.

Get Set

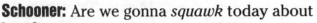

Hello! Everybody treating each other well out there? I hope so! Because God made it very clear that he expects us to love each other. It's a message we all need to be reminded of from time to time. Isn't that right, Schooner? *Schooner pops up.*

Schooner: Are we gonna *squawk* today about love?
Leader: You mean talk, Schooner?
Schooner: One and the same, boss.
Leader: Yes we are.
Schooner: *(turns away)* Yuck. I don't like all that kissy love stuff.
Leader: Love is more than that, Schooner.
Schooner: Nah. I don't think so.
Leader: Sure it is. Parents love their children.
Schooner: *(silence—cocks head)*
Leader: Children love their families.
Schooner: *(silence—cocks head the other way)*
Leader: Leaders love their parrots.
Schooner: *(sits up alert)* That's love?
Leader: Sure.
Schooner: And that's only natural, boss.
Leader:: I suppose so, Schooner.
Schooner: Everyone knows birds are naturally lovable.
Leader: I can see that.
Schooner: You can hug 'em, too, just not too hard.
Leader: No, not too hard.
Schooner: And one more thing.
Leader: Yes?
Schooner: If you care to hug a bird…very, very gently…you can feel its heart beat.
Leader: Can I try?
Schooner: *(Leader places his/her hand on Schooner's breast)*
Leader:: That's a lot of little love beats!
Schooner: Ok, boss.
Leader: Ok what?
Schooner: We can talk about l-o-v-e.
Leader: Thank you, Schooner. In today's Bible story we'll hear more about God's Ten Commandments.
Schooner: Rules that help us get along.
Leader: Precisely, Schooner.
Schooner: So name a few, please.

Leader: Let's start with Mom and Dad.
Schooner: A good place to start, boss.
Leader: God wants us to treat our parents with love and respect.
Schooner: What does that mean…respect?
Leader: To listen to and to give special attention. To honor.
Schooner: Parents are special people.
Leader: God thinks so, Schooner.
Schooner: Did you know that my parents named me Schooner?
Leader: Parents like to name their children.
Schooner: My name is as old as the sea.
Leader: How's that?
Schooner: I had relatives on the Mayflower.
Leader: One of the first ships to come to America?
Schooner: Yup.
Leader: You are an old bird.
Schooner: But I'm also a lovebird, remember?
Leader: Of course. God wants us to treat each other with love.
Schooner: And how do we do that, boss?
Leader: Caring for them and their things.
Schooner: Like…
Leader: Speaking the truth about them.
Schooner: Go on.
Leader: And not taking what isn't ours.
Schooner: What if you just want to borrow something for a day?
Leader: God's law is clear. No borrowing without permission.
Schooner: So all you need is love?
Leader: God's love, Schooner, to help us love others.
Schooner: I hear you, boss.
Leader: I'm glad you do. Let's hear all about it up next in Bible 4U!

1 Bible 4U!

Welcome to Bible 4U! theater where the story of what happened at Mt. Sinai continues. When we left the scene, an eyewitness was telling how Moses met God atop the mountain. Smoke billowed up from the mountain while lightning and thunder shook the whole place. The nation of Israel waited at the base of the mountain, quaking with fear. Only Moses could approach God, and the people were glad for that. In fact, they begged Moses to talk to God and tell them what God said. They feared that if God talked to them directly, they'd die.

Moses approached the mountain where God waited for him in thick darkness. God gave Moses the Ten Commandments—rules that would make the Israelites his own special people. They would ignore all the fake gods people around them worshiped. They would love God above everything, treat his name with great care, and worship him on a special day. Now the list of commandments goes on. Our friend Amariah is back to share his childhood experiences at Mount Sinai with a young brother and sister who have just become his friends.

Scenes from Sinai
Based on Exodus 20, 31:18

Elihu: Would you come home with us, Amariah? I know my mom and dad would love to meet you.

Adina: Please come with us. Our mom makes the best mutton stew.

Elihu: And I'm sure she has warm flat bread right out of the oven…

Adina: And figs and date cakes…

Amariah: *(laughing)* I surrender. I'll come!

Elihu: Cool!

Adina: Mom and Dad will be so happy to meet someone who was there the day God met Moses on the holy mountain and gave him the Ten Commandments.

Amariah: Do you remember the commandments I told you about so far?

Elihu: Yep! God wants us to love him more than anyone. And because we love him, we're to be careful how we use his name.

Adina: And he wants us to set aside a special day to worship him and rest.

Amariah: *(ruffling their hair)* I'm proud of you two. You were really listening.

Adina: So, tell us more. I mean, we've heard all this since we were little, but it's different coming from you.

Amariah: There's nothing I'd rather do than talk about God's law! You remember well that the first commandments tell us how to treat God. The other commandments tell us how to treat other people.

Elihu: *(turning up his nose)* That wouldn't include sisters, would it?

Amariah: It would. And brothers too.

Adina: Aw, man!

Amariah: But the very next commandment tells about moms and dads. We're supposed to honor them.

Elihu: What exactly does that mean?

Amariah: Well, it might look something like this. Instead of, *(in a nasal, whiny voice)* "Oh, Mom, do I *have* to?" you would say, "Sure, Mom. You look tired. Is there anything else I can do?"

Elihu: Whoa.

Amariah: *And,* it means talking to our parents respectfully and treating them like they're important to you.

Adina: I'm not always very good at that.

Amariah: *(smiling fondly)* If you trust God he will help you, little one.

Adina: That's good. I need a lot of help.

Elihu: You can say that again.

Adina: Hey!

Amariah: Remember what I said about this including brothers and sisters?

Elihu and Adina: Oops.

Amariah: That's okay. I had a sister too once.

Elihu: Was she a pain?

Amariah: About as often as I was. *(Adina gives her brother an overly sweet smile.)*

Elihu: *(clears his throat)* Anyway, tell us more.

Amariah: If we honor others, we won't lie, steal, hurt them or want to take anything that's theirs.

Adina: That pretty well covers it.

Elihu: But sometimes people are just down-right nasty. There's this kid in our tribe who plays mean tricks on people all the time. Once he killed a bunch of flies and put them in our jar of drinking water.

Amariah: Tell me, Elihu, does God love this boy?

Elihu: I guess. Well, yeah. Probably.

Amariah: God didn't say following the Ten Commandments would be easy. He just told us to do it.

Adina: So what did Moses look like?

Amariah: His face glowed from being in the presence of God. It is an awesome thing to be the bridge between God and his people.

Elihu: I guess! What if you had been the one to talk to God?

Amariah: Oh—none of us wanted to do that. We were scared. The very mountain trembled when God came down. I would have fallen apart! Moses was the man God picked for the job. I'm glad.

Elihu: It's so cool that you saw this happen.

Amariah: I'm an old man now. Will you tell my story to others when I'm gone?

Elihu: We'd love to! But you'll be with us for a long time, I pray.

Amariah: Thank you. An old man can always use a few more good prayers. Now, what about that dinner you promised me?

Elihu: Come on! Our house is over here.

Adina: I get to sit by him at the table.

Elihu: Do not.

Adina: Do too.

Elihu: Do not.

Happily, Adina and Elihu grab Amariah's hands and lead him from the room.

How cool would it be to meet an eyewitness like Amariah? I'm glad we got to share this story today. Here are a few questions comin' your way!

Toss the four numbered balls to different parts of the room. Bring the kids with the balls to the front one-by-one and ask these questions. Allow kids to get help from the group if they need it. After each correct answer, let kids drop the ball into a bag.

 ■ **What are the first four commandments about?**

 ■ **What are the rest of the commandments about?**

 ■ **Why were these commandments so important to God's people?**

 ■ **Suppose everyone lived by these commandments. How would our world be different?**

If you look around, you'll find parts of the Ten Commandments everywhere. Most of our laws are grounded in the Ten Commandments. In fact, most laws around the world are! That's why this Scripture is so important to us.

Bible Verse
If you really keep the royal law found in Scripture, "Love your neighbor as yourself," you are doing right. James 2:8

Think about this for a minute: What makes us a nation? We live here, we salute the same flag, we have a government, we say the same pledge of allegiance. One reason God gave the Ten Commandments was to make the Israelites into a nation—his nation! He wanted to make them different from all the other tribes and nations that lived back them. He wanted them to be an example to other people, to show what it's like when a whole nation honors God and honors others.

Today God's kingdom includes people from many nations. But just like the Israelites of Moses' time, living in ways that honor God and honor others shines a bright example of how God wants things to be on his earth. If you believe in God, you're part of his kingdom. If you treat others with love, you draw them toward God's kingdom too. And that's just about the best thing anyone can do. Today in your shepherd groups you'll learn more about what it means to love others.

Dismiss kids to their small groups.

2 Shepherd's Spot

Gather your small group and help them find Exodus 20 in their Bibles. Have a volunteer read Exodus 20:12–21.

■ **What do all these commandments have in common?** *(They talk about how to treat other people.)*

Hundreds of years after this, Jesus taught that the two most important commandments are to "Love the Lord your God with all your heart and with all your soul and with all your mind" and to "Love your neighbor as yourself." That's in the book of Matthew in the New Testament. Jesus taught that the commandments were important, but doing the right thing is only part of obeying. He wants us to do the right things because our hearts are full of his love.

Let's make another set of "Steps to Obedience" so we can remember the rules God gave his people to teach them how to love each other.

Distribute the "Steps to Obedience 2" handout, (p. 104). Have kids fold it in half on the dotted line and cut the dark lines between the dots. Lay the paper flat again, then valley fold on the middle line and mountain fold on the two dashed lines.

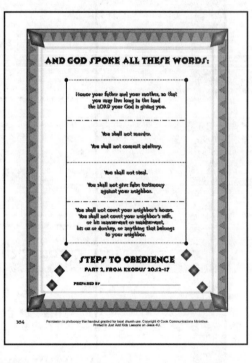

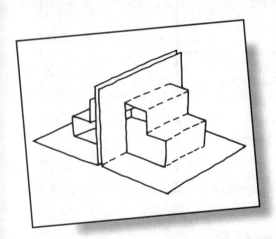

Pull the steps forward. If you wish, let kids add a backing sheet of construction paper. If they've completed the first "Steps of Obedience" from Lesson 9, encourage them to glue the two completed steps back to back as shown in the diagram above.

■ **Can you keep all these commandments and still not really love others? Explain.**

Loving God is first, loving people is second. It's not so hard to love our wonderful God, but sometimes it's hard to love people. When I pause in my prayer, think silently of someone you need God's help to love. Then I'll finish my prayer. Pause to pray. **Dear heavenly Father, your commandments guide us and teach us how to get along. Sometimes it's really hard. We ask you to fill our hearts with love for these people.** Pause here for your kids petition, praises or prayer requests. **Thank you for guiding us and loving us even though we don't deserve it. In Jesus' name, amen.**

AND GOD SPOKE ALL THESE WORDS:

Honor your father and your mother, so that
you may live long in the land
the LORD your God is giving you.

You shall not murder.

You shall not commit adultery.

You shall not steal.

You shall not give false testimony
against your neighbor.

You shall not covet your neighbor's house.
You shall not covet your neighbor's wife,
or his manservant or maidservant,
his ox or donkey, or anything that belongs
to your neighbor.

STEPS TO OBEDIENCE
PART 2, FROM EXODUS 20:12–17

PREPARED BY _____

Workshop Wonders

The Ten Commandments written on stone tablets were a solid reminder to God's people of their experience with God near Mount Sinai. Thunder rumbled, lightning flashed and trumpet blasts told of his almighty presence. The Israelites had seen God's presence guiding them with a pillar of cloud by day and a pillar of fire by night. Now they experienced God's presence in a different way.

Get List:
- ☐ Bibles
- ☐ graham crackers
- ☐ vanilla frosting
- ☐ fruit leather
- ☐ kitchen shears
- ☐ drinking straws
- ☐ fruit ring cereal
- ☐ decorator gel tubes
- ☐ plates, napkins, plastic knives

■ Why do you think God appeared in smoke and fire on the mountain? What other elements would you choose?

God cared for the Israelites and wanted them to turn to him and to treat each other with love and respect. The Ten Commandments were the best way to make sure everyone, rich and poor, young and old, would be treated the same fair way under God's authority. Let's make a tablet snack to enjoy remembering this momentous occasion in Israelite history.

Distribute paper plates and two graham cracker rectangles (the full piece) to each student. Place crackers on the plate long side to long side. **Here are your stone tablets.** Ask kids to open their Bibles and read Exodus 20:12–21; 31:18.

■ If God asked you to help design the Ten Commandment tablets, what special touches would you add?
■ When can you find time this week to reread the commandments and press them in your heart?

God did not want his commandments about loving others kept only in stone, but also in the hearts and minds of all who loved him. He wanted them to keep the commandments in their hearts, so they were as close to a person as his or her own thoughts. Turn your stone tablets into a writing tablet with reminders to love our neighbor.

Use the shears to cut two pieces of fruit leather slightly smaller than the graham crackers. Snip the drinking straws in half and distribute. Have kids take the cut-straw and use it to hole punch the pieces of fruit leather five times down the long end of each piece. Spread frosting on the crackers. Gently press the fruit leather onto the frosted graham cracker (holes to the middle) forcing a bit of frosting out each hole. Stick a fruit circle onto each hole for pages-in-a-tablet look. Use the gel tubes to write "love my neighbor" on the tablets. **Now you have a tablet of God's truth!** Kids can share their thoughts on treating others in love as they enjoy their snacks.

If you wish to provide more options for your kids, set out a jar of peanut butter (check for peanut allergies) in place of the frosting, sliced cheese for the fruit leather and oat circles for the fruit cereal.

Fold down the corners to start your paper airplane.

SPECIAL DELIVERY

TO

Love and honor God.

What does it mean to have God's commandments written on your heart?

Why did God give these rules to his people?

Today at church we learned the Ten Commandments.

It may seem impossible to follow God's command to love one another. Cold and selfish hearts are sure to get in the way. Fill a glass half full with water and drop in an ice cube. Try to use a string to pick up the cube—without touching the cube. Impossible? God did not give us commandments we couldn't keep. Sprinkle on a little salt and wait ten minutes. Now lift the string. (The salt melts the ice, trapping the string once it refreezes.) God's rules help us along. Stick to 'em!

Bible Verse

"Love the Lord your God with all your heart and with all your soul and with all your mind." This is the first and greatest commandment. Matthew: 22:37-38

◊ Where is it easier to love one another—at home or at school? Explain.

Family FUN

Live It!

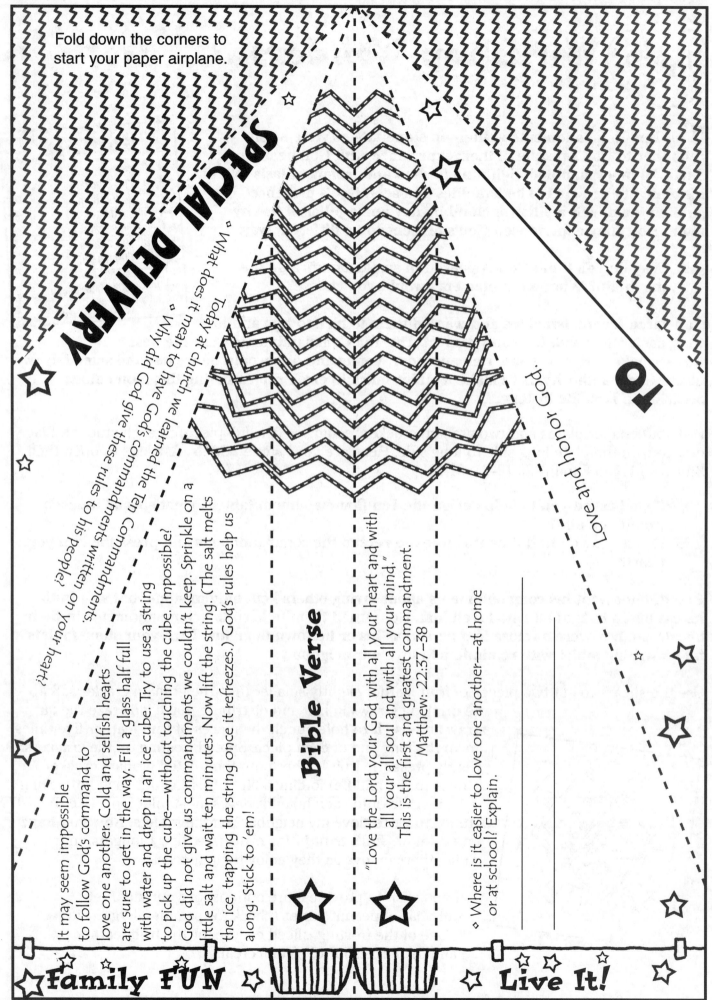

All the Best

Option

Get Set
LARGE GROUP ■ Greet kids and do a puppet skit. Schooner receives a present and learns about giving freely and with joy.

❑ large bird puppet ❑ puppeteer

1 Bible 4U! Instant Drama
LARGE GROUP ■ Three sparkling "gifts" to the tabernacle share the excitement of being used in God's house.

❑ 3 actors ❑ copies of pp. 110–111, Shine On! script ❑ 4 numbered balls ❑ bag
Optional: ❑ blanket ❑ plastic jewels

2 Shepherd's Spot
SMALL GROUP ■ Make giving boxes to remind kids to give freely because they've received generous gifts from God's hand. Share concerns and pray together. Send home the Special Delivery handout.

❑ Bibles ❑ pencils ❑ scissors ❑ glue sticks ❑ copies of p. 114, Giving Box
❑ copies of p. 116, Special Delivery

Option

Workshop Wonders
SMALL GROUP ■ Make simple tabernacle Arks filled with treats for kids to give away.

❑ paper lunch bags ❑ tissue or newspaper ❑ markers ❑ gold glitter glue
❑ gold and silver wrapped candy ❑ "spiced" tea bags ❑ potpourri ❑ glue-on
jewels ❑ blue, purple or red yarn ❑ extra candy for snacking Optional: ❑ angel
stickers ❑ tent

Bible Basis
The Tabernacle
Exodus 25:1–9,
40:34–38

Learn It!
We all have
something to
give to God's
kingdom.

Live It!
Give with
a glad heart.

Bible Verse
Freely you have
received, freely give.
Matthew 10:8

Quick Takes

Exodus 25:1–9, 40:34–38

The Lord said to Moses,
2 "Tell the Israelites to bring me an offering. You are to receive the offering for me from each man whose heart prompts him to give.
3 These are the offerings you are to receive from them: gold, silver and bronze;
4 blue, purple and scarlet yarn and fine linen; goat hair;
5 ram skins dyed red and hides of sea cows; acacia wood;
6 olive oil for the light; spices for the anointing oil and for the fragrant incense;
7 and onyx stones and other gems to be mounted on the ephod and breastpiece.
8 "Then have them make a sanctuary for me, and I will dwell among them.
9 Make this tabernacle and all its furnishings exactly like the pattern I will show you.
40:34 Then the cloud covered the Tent of Meeting, and the glory of the Lord filled the tabernacle.
35 Moses could not enter the Tent of Meeting because the cloud had settled upon it, and the glory of the Lord filled the tabernacle.
36 In all the travels of the Israelites, whenever the cloud lifted from above the tabernacle, they would set out;
37 but if the cloud did not lift, they did not set out—until the day it lifted.
38 So the cloud of the Lord was over the tabernacle by day, and fire was in the cloud by night, in the sight of all the house of Israel during all their travels.

Insights

God asked for offerings from his people to be used in building a house of worship—a place where God would be present with them. He didn't ask for the kinds of things we bag up and take to charities. He asked for their very best—gold, silver, jewels, fine linen and animal hides, beautiful wood, olive oil and fragrant spices. How would former slaves have such things? They received them from the Egyptians the night of the Exodus.

As the people came forward with their treasures, imagine the piles of riches. Gems glittered in the brilliant desert sun. Piles of beautiful cloth and purple yarn. Rich smelling spices. Jars of precious oil. The best and finest of all they possessed grew in piles before the priests as the offerings came in. Look at all God had done for them! Now they could give something in return. God told Moses, "You are to receive the offering for me from each man whose heart prompts him to give" (Exodus 25:2). These were heart gifts.

Today heart gifts come in both tangible and intangible varieties. It's marvelous for children to form giving habits when they're young. But intangibles are just as important—gifts of time, concern, helpfulness. And while kids don't have piles of money, they do have open, unselfish hearts. Help them understand that some of the most precious riches we can give are not those we can see or touch. We can be generous with our time, with understanding a troubled person, with a sincere spirit of encouragement.

Our gifts of the heart reflect God's generosity. He wants to dwell with us, in us, and use us in his kingdom. Use this lesson to teach kids that their gifts to God are important, and that everyone has something to give.

"Option" Get Set

Bring to class a handsome tie or kerchief to give to Schooner. Put it in your pocket or place it out of sight for now.

Hey there! Do you know what you look like to me? Like a group of kids who have something great to give to God's kingdom! From the smallest of you to the tallest. Speaking of small, has anyone seen a little bird around here? *Schooner pops up.*

Schooner: *Squawk!* I'm not so small.
Leader: You're a little smaller than I am.

Schooner: But I'm special!
Leader: You sure are. That's why I have a present for you today.

Schooner: For me?
Leader: *(looks around)* I don't see any other parrot in the room.

Schooner: It's not my birthday.
Leader: No, it's not.

Schooner: It's not my flying anniversary.
Leader: Right again.

Schooner: It's not "Take a Parrot to Work" Day.
Leader: Hadn't heard about that one, Schooner.

Schooner: Don't worry. I marked your calendar for next year.
Leader: How thoughtful of you.

Schooner: So why a present?
Leader: God wants us to give with a glad heart.

Schooner: Today?
Leader: Any day. And it doesn't have to be a birthday.

Schooner: Well, I'll be a chicken's uncle!
Leader: *(tie the handsome tie or kerchief around Schooner's neck.)*

Schooner: I'm squawkless, boss.
Leader: *(leans in to the group)* That's a first.

Schooner: *(looks glum)* I don't have anything to give you.
Leader: Oh, yes you do.

Schooner: *(looks around)* I didn't bring anything.
Leader: Yes you did.

Schooner: What?
Leader: *(pats Schooner.)* You, Schooner. You're my gift.

Schooner: But that's not enough.
Leader: It is. Your happy heart makes my heart glad.

Schooner: Well, shucks. I *am* a pretty good egg.
Leader: Of course.

Schooner: Why just the other day, this little birdie flew in…
Leader: *(rolls eyes)* Here we go!

Schooner: …and asked me to pose for an ice sculpture.
Leader: An ice sculpture, you say.

Schooner: I'd have to work in a freezer, though.
Leader: Really?

Schooner: Or I'd drip.
Leader: A drip—with feathers.

Schooner: I've said it before, boss. It's a gift.
Leader: In today's Bible story God asks his people to give gifts of gold, silver and jewels for his tabernacle.

Schooner: Table what?
Leader: Tabernacle. Think of it as a church, Schooner, a special place to worship God.

Schooner: Jewels and gold? Expensive stuff.
Leader: They were offerings—things given with a glad heart.

Schooner: To whom?
Leader: To God. God's people gave the best they had because God was—and is—worthy of all honor, glory and respect.

Schooner: *(ponders)* The best they had, huh?
Leader: Today, we can give God precious things like our talents, the things we're good at.

Schooner: And a glad heart is a great gift.
Leader: Worth all the gold in the world.

Schooner: I want to give like that—freely, like God gives to us.
Leader: Right on, Schooner.

Schooner: *(looks at the gift around his neck)* Thanks, boss.
Leader: You're very welcome, Schooner.

One Happy Parrot: Bible 4U! up next.

1 Bible 4U!

Welcome to today's edition of Bible 4U! theater. Today we're going to hear from a bunch of gems. Even as we speak, the Israelites are piling gifts before the priests. I see beautiful cloth, soft animal hides, rich purple yarns, jars of precious olive oil and piles of sparkling jewels. This can mean only one thing: the people are bringing gifts.

God has asked Moses to tell the people to bring gifts for a very special purpose. They're going to build a special house, a tabernacle where God's spirit will be with them. They will worship God there, and offer sacrifices. God didn't make people bring gifts. He only wanted gifts that people would give from their hearts. Skilled crafts people would take the handsome gifts and make a beautiful tent. They would also make a gold-covered box to go inside the tent and hold the tablets on which God wrote the Ten Commandments.

Let's catch the action as the pile of gifts grows and grows.

Instant Prep

Choose three girls to play Goldy, Gem and Twinkle. Give them each a copy of the "Shine On!" script below. If you have a blanket on hand, have them huddle under it during the opening part of the script.

for Overachievers

Have a five-person drama team prepare the story. Dress the three "gems" in bright jewel tones. Have two extras dressed in black. Have them pull off the blanket at the appropriate spot in the story and toss plastic "jewels" when the script calls for it.

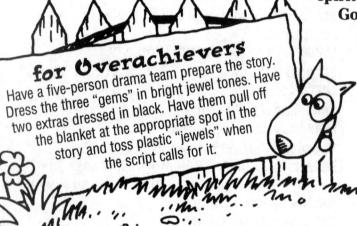

Shine On!
Based on Exodus 25, 40

Goldy: It's dark in here. Doesn't anyone else get tired of this gloomy little box?

Gem: I do, Goldy. We haven't seen the sun in months. How 'bout you, Twinkle?

Twinkle: How am I supposed to twinkle in the dark? We haven't been out of this box since the night we left Egypt. Do you remember?

Goldy: Oh boy, do I. My little golden heart beat like a brass drum.

Gem: Everyone was crying.

Twinkle: Well, they had a reason. Pharaoh didn't let the Israelites go, so all the first born children of Egypt died. The Egyptians couldn't wait for the Israelites to leave.

Goldy: That's when we started our great adventure. At least we thought it was going to be a great adventure.

Gem: I never thought our mistress would give us away like that. Remember how she just shoved us into the hands of an Israelite? She said, "Take my gold and jewels and leave!"

Twinkle: Then we got stuffed into this box.

Goldy: But it didn't turn out be such a great adventure after all. Sure, we've traveled a lot with our new Israelite family, but they never, like, put us on or anything.

Gem: So here we sit in the dark, dark, dark!

Bummer, bummer...BUMMER!

All: *(covering their eyes as darkness gives way to bright light)* Whoa*! (They all blink and squint.)*

Twinkle: Don't look now, girls, but I think things are changing.

Goldy: Look at you, Gem. You're gorgeous in the sunlight!

Gem: Ahhh...I'm shining! I'm shining!

Gems jostle back and forth as if they're being carried.

Twinkle: Not only that, you're going somewhere. We're all going somewhere. I wonder what's up?

Goldy: *(a little frightened)* Whatever it is, I hope we can stay together.

Gem: Hang on, girls. I think we're about to get dumped into a...

All: *(as if they're falling)* Aaaaaaaa!

They slap their hands on the floor loudly, as if they've hit bottom.

Gem: *(breathless)* ...dumped into a pile!

Twinkle: Goldy, are you there?

Goldy: I'm here, Twinkle. How 'bout you, Gem? Are you still with us?

Gem: I'm over here. In a huge pile of...

Twinkle: Gems and precious stones...

Goldy: ...and gold and silver. Wowzers!

Gem: What's all this about? Is it going to be better than being stuck in that little wooden box?

Twinkle: Oh, yeah. It's going to be better.

Gem: Watch out! Here come more jewels!

All: Ow! *(They rub their heads as if something's just been dropped on them.)*

Goldy: What did you mean about it being better, Twinkle?

Twinkle: I heard that goldsmith over there talking. People are giving all their treasures to build a tabernacle where they can worship God. They're going to use us to make beautiful things.

Gem: Really?

Twinkle: Really. They want to honor God because he brought them out of slavery in Egypt.

Goldy: We remember all about that!

Twinkle: They'll worship him in this beautiful tabernacle—and we'll be part of it!

Gem: No kidding! This is gonna' be *awesome!*

Goldy: They must really love God. I mean, people don't usually give treasures like us away. Are you sure somebody didn't make them give all this stuff?

Twinkle: God's people gave because they wanted to. They gave their very best.

Gem: *(awed)* And now we'll be made into something beautiful. And we'll be in the presence of God!

Twinkle: I'm gonna' shine like I've never shone before.

Goldy: My gold will gleam softly as the people worship God.

Twinkle: I'm so glad our Israelite family gave us for this. It's an honor.

Goldy: They gave their best.

Gem: And we'll look our best. Whatever they do with us, we'll shine with all our might.

Twinkle: Look, Goldy! The goldsmith is about to take you. *(Waves and shouts)* 'Bye! I just know he'll make you into something absolutely wonderful!

Goldy: 'Bye! See you in the tabernacle. *(She exits.)*

Gem: Hey—it looks like it's our turn.

Twinkle: He-e-e-re we go.

Gem: Shine on, Twinkle!

Twinkle: Only our best for God!

The jewels exit.

Well, that was a sparkling bunch of characters. How 'bout you guys? Here's your chance to shine!

Toss the four numbered balls to different parts of the room. Bring the kids with the balls to the front one-by-one and ask these questions. Allow kids to get help from the group if they need it. After each correct answer, let kids drop the ball into a bag.

 ■ What was a tabernacle, and why were they building it?

 ■ Where did the Israelites get those gems and jewels?

 ■ How do you think God's people felt about parting with such treasures?

 ■ How do you know when a gift comes straight from someone's heart?

The Israelites had seen God do incredible things for them. First there were the plagues God sent to persuade the Egyptians to let his people go. I'll bet you can remember some of them. Let children call them out. Finally, after all the firstborn children of Egypt died, Pharaoh set the Israelites free. Pharaoh's armies came after them, but God helped them escape through the Red Sea. God fed them with manna and quail from the sky, and gave them water from a rock in the desert. And he gave them his commandments on Mt. Sinai. That's quite a list!

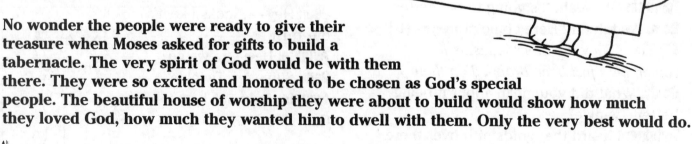

Bible Verse
Freely you have received, freely give.
Matthew 10:8

No wonder the people were ready to give their treasure when Moses asked for gifts to build a tabernacle. The very spirit of God would be with them there. They were so excited and honored to be chosen as God's special people. The beautiful house of worship they were about to build would show how much they loved God, how much they wanted him to dwell with them. Only the very best would do.

 **Today in your shepherd groups, you'll talk more about giving God your best!**

Dismiss kids to their small groups.

2 Shepherd's Spot

Gather kids in your small group and help them find Exodus 25 in their Bibles.

Take a look at yourselves—what you're wearing, what you're carrying.

- **What's the most expensive thing you have right now? Suppose I said, "I'm your teacher and I want that. Fork it over." Would you give it to me? How would you feel about it?**

- **Suppose I said, "This little kid, just about your size, wandered into the church. She's homeless and her clothes are all torn and dirty. She doesn't know where her parents are. What can we do for her?" How would you respond?**

That's the difference between giving because you have to and giving from the heart. God had done so much for the Israelite people. Now he wanted them to build a church or a tabernacle, a place where they could worship him and where he could be with them. He told Moses to ask for gifts so they could make everything they'd need for the tabernacle. But he didn't make anyone give. God wanted heart gifts. Let's read about it straight from the Bible. Invite volunteers to read Exodus 25:1-9.

When you're part of God's family, the giving never stops. Let's make a cool box that reminds us why we give.

Distribute the "Giving Box" handout (p. 114) and lead kids through the assembly steps given on the handout. Invite a volunteer to read Matthew 10:8 from the side of the box. Ask kids to discuss what they've "received freely" from God and what they can "freely give." **Keep your box as a reminder to give freely because you love God. You may want to put in coins or notes about heart gifts.**

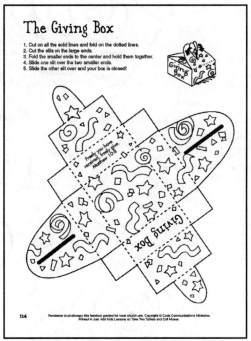

The Giving Box

1. Cut on all the solid lines and fold on the dotted lines.
2. Cut the slits on the large ends.
3. Fold the smaller ends to the center and hold them together.
4. Slide one slit over the two smaller ends.
5. Slide the other slit over and your box is closed!

As we close with prayer, I'm going to pause and let you give thanks for what God has given you. Dear Lord, we know that all we have comes from your hand. We thank you for (pause for kids to respond). **Give us generous hearts that reflect your love to everyone around us. In Jesus name, amen.**

The Giving Box

1. Cut on all the solid lines and fold on the dotted lines.
2. Cut the slits on the large ends.
3. Fold the smaller ends to the center and hold them together.
4. Slide one slit over the two smaller ends.
5. Slide the other slit over and your box is closed!

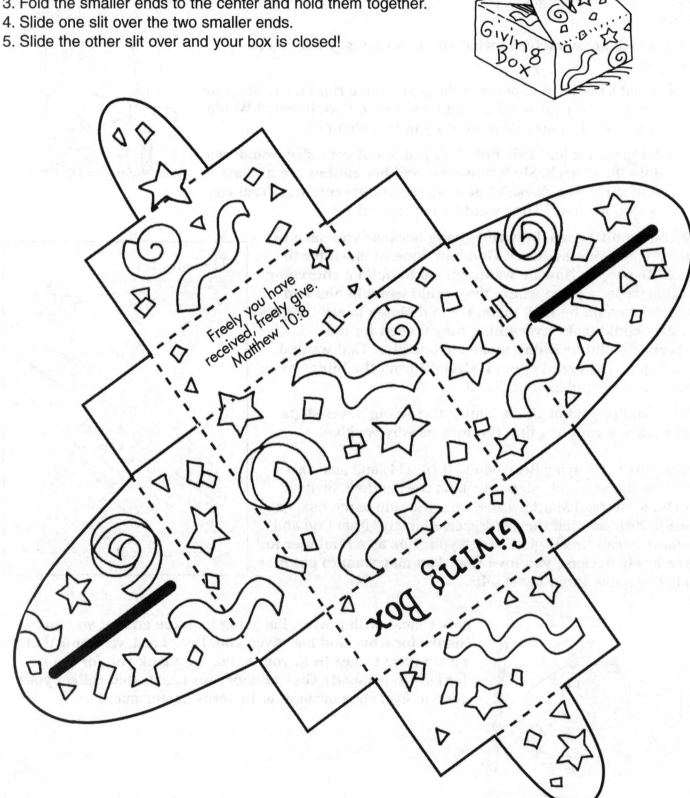

Freely you have received, freely give.
Matthew 10:8

Giving Box

Workshop Wonders

If you have an easy-to-assemble tent, bring it to class and set it up. This will be the "tabernacle" for kids to sit inside after they make their paper Arks.

Imagine the most special place on earth. More wonderful than an amusement park or a sports stadium. Think of a beautiful tent draped with purple cloth, sparkling with gold and gems in the midday sun.

We've learned how the Israelite people gave gifts to build a tabernacle where the spirit of God would be with his people. It was the place where the Israelites worshiped God, and the instructions for building it came from none other than God himself!

Get List:
- ☐ paper lunch bags
- ☐ tissue paper
- ☐ markers
- ☐ gold glitter glue
- ☐ gold and silver wrapped candy
- ☐ "spiced" tea bags
- ☐ potpourri
- ☐ glue-on jewels
- ☐ blue, purple or red yarn
- ☐ extra candy for snacking

Optional:
- ☐ angel stickers
- ☐ tent

- ■ **Where do you go to worship God? Does it always need to be in church? Explain.**
- ■ **If our church appointed you "top church builder" for the day, what suggestions would you make for the most beautiful church ever?**

And only the best would do! God asked the people to give precious gold, silver and gems. And he told Moses how to make the Ark of Covenant, a gold covered box to hold the stone tablets of the Ten Commandments as well as a jar of manna. The Ark of the Covenant was a precious box made to hold precious things. Let make models of the Ark of the Covenant and fill them with special things too to remember today's Bible story.

Give two lunch bags to each student. Have them write today's Bible verse on bag #1.
"Freely you have received, freely give. Matthew 10:8"

Stuff bag #2 with tissue or crumpled newspaper. Drop in some gold and silver wrapped treats (offerings of gold and silver), spiced tea (spices for the anointing oil) or potpourri (fragrant incense). Now slide bag #1 (with the Bible Verse) over bag #2 to make the box. Have kids adhere the angel stickers on top of the bag, one on each end. Glue on jewels and blue, purple or red yarn swirls. Fill the empty spaces with glitter glue. Sprinkle the bag with additional gold glitter.

- ■ **The Israelites honored God because he took care of them. What makes you want to honor God?**
- ■ **Besides things you can touch, what "heart gifts" can you offer God?**

We all have something to give God's kingdom. Remember that each of us is a precious one-of-a-kind creation. No two alike! God asks that we give our gifts freely.

If you set up a tent before class, have kids sit inside and eat their snacks. Ask kids to discuss whether they wish to keep their golden boxes or give them away.

Fold down the corners to start your paper airplane.

SPECIAL DELIVERY

TO

Give with a glad heart.

Today at church we learned how the Israelites gave gifts to build a tabernacle where they could worship God.

"Share the highlights of today's story with your family."

"What's the most precious thing you've ever given to God?"

Make a simple model of the table used to carry the Ark of the Covenant that was kept inside the tabernacle. Lay two empty paper towel tubes side by side. Glue wide craft sticks on top and decorate it. Paint your tabletop gold or spread glue and sprinkle it with gold glitter. If you made a model of the Ark of the Covenant at church, place it on your table. Or use the table to hold something else that reminds you that God is always with you.

Bible Verse

Freely you have received, freely give.
Matthew 10:8

◇ What gift, freely given, have you received that made you smile?

◇ Is your gift storytelling? Start with the words "Once upon a time" and share today's story with a brother, sister or friend.

Family FUN

Live It!

Lesson 12

Faithful to the End

Option

Get Set
LARGE GROUP ■ Greet kids and do a puppet skit. Schooner "wings it" as he learns about ordinary people who serve God faithfully.

❏ large bird puppet ❏ puppeteer

1

Bible 4U! Instant Drama
LARGE GROUP ■ A reporter interviews the fascinating walking stick family as they tell about Moses passing leadership to Joshua.

❏ four actors ❏ copies of pp. 120–121, A Wonderful Life script ❏ 4 numbered balls
❏ bag Optional: ❏ burlap to wrap the "walking stick" actors

2

Shepherd's Spot
SMALL GROUP ■ Make a fun pop-up card to give to a person who's been a great leader and encourager. Share concerns and pray together. Send home the Special Delivery handout.

❏ Bibles ❏ pencils ❏ scissors ❏ glue sticks ❏ copies of p. 124, Love That Leader
❏ copies of p. 126, Special Delivery

Option

Workshop Wonders
SMALL GROUP ■ Walking sticks keep the pace with today's Bible story.

❏ dry, sturdy tree branches ❏ fine sandpaper ❏ acrylic paints and brushes ❏ twine
Optional: ❏ wrapping paper rolls ❏ feathers ❏ pinecones ❏ beads ❏ ribbon

Bible Basis
Moses passes leadership to Joshua.
Numbers 27:12–22;
Deuteronomy 34:1–7, 10–11

Learn It!
God uses ordinary people to do amazing things.

Live It!
Serve God faithfully.

Bible Verse
For the Lord loves the just and will not forsake this faithful ones.
Psalm 37:28

117

Quick Takes

Then the Lord said to Moses, "Go up this mountain in the Abarim Range and see the land I have given the Israelites.

13 After you have seen it, you too will be gathered to your people, as your brother Aaron was.

14 for when the community rebelled at the waters in the Desert of Zin, both of you disobeyed my command to honor me as holy before their eyes." (These were the waters of Meribah Kadesh, in the Desert of Zin.)

15 Moses said to the Lord,

16 "May the Lord, the God of the spirits of all mankind, appoint a man over this community

17 to go out and come in before them, one who will lead them out and bring them in, so that the Lord's people will not be like sheep without a shepherd."

18 So the Lord said to Moses, "Take Joshua son of Nun, a man in whom is the spirit, and lay your hand on him.

19 Make him stand before Eleazar the priest and the entire assembly and commission him in their presence.

20 Give him some of your authority so that the whole Israelite community will obey him.

21 He is to stand before Eleazar the priest, who will obtain decisions for him by enquiring of the Urim before the Lord. At his command he and the entire community of the Israelites will go out, and at his command they will come in."

22 Moses did as the Lord commanded him. He took Joshua and made him stand before Eleazar the priest and the whole assembly.

Deuteronomy 34:1 Then Moses climbed Mount Nebo from the plains of Moab to the top of Pisgah, across from Jericho. There the Lord showed him the whole land—from Gilead to Dan,

2 all of Naphtali, the territory of Ephraim and Manasseh, all the land of Judah as far as the western sea,

3 the Negev and the whole region from the Valley of Jericho, the City of Palms, as far as Zoar.

4 Then the Lord said to him, "This is the land I promised on oath to Abraham, Isaac and Jacob when I said, 'I will give it to your descendants.' I have let you see it with your eyes, but you will not cross over into it."

5 And Moses the servant of the Lord died there in Moab, as the Lord had said.

6 He buried him in Moab, in the valley opposite Beth Peor, but to this day no one knows where his grave is.

7 Moses was a hundred and twenty years old when he died, yet his eyes were not weak nor his strength gone.

10 Since then, no prophet has risen in Israel like Moses, whom the Lord knew face to face,

11 who did all those miraculous signs and wonders the Lord sent him to do in Egypt to Pharaoh and to all his officials and to his whole land.

Insights

Moses' remarkable life comes to an end, and with it an era in the history of God's people. No greater tribute can be given to this man than the one in Deuteronomy 34:10: "Since then, no prophet has risen in Israel like Moses, whom the Lord knew face to face."

After forty years of wandering in the desert, the Israelites were about to cross into the Promised Land. Joshua was the rising star among the sons of Israel, and Moses passed the mantel of leadership to him. Moses' was God's man. Three thousand years later, his faithfulness still shines as an inspiration and example.

Moses' relationship with God was unique to that time for God's purposes. But we can know God. With open souls and seeking hearts, we can be known by God and used for his purposes today. We don't have to be remarkable in any way except our devotion and faithfulness.

And the same goes for your kids. Use this lesson to challenge kids to know God and to live faithfully. Help them understand that God still uses faithful people in extraordinary ways.

Get Set

Hello and goodbye! No—don't leave yet. I'm just getting you ready for what happens in today's Bible story We'll say goodbye to Moses, one of the greatest prophets who ever lived. God said so himself. But before we do that, let's say hello to our favorite parrot. *Schooner pops up.*

Schooner: Did I hear my name?

Leader: Hello!

Schooner: I like "hellos."

Leader: They're the best part of my day.

Schooner: So it's a little sad, then.

Leader: What is, Schooner?

Schooner: To say goodbye to Moses.

Leader: Oh, yes. We've spent a lot of time talking about Moses, haven't we?

Schooner: Yup.

Leader: God loved Moses.

Schooner: Moses' taught me a lot of things, too.

Leader: Share with us, Schooner.

Schooner: Moses taught me to trust and listen to God. That God sends us helper, to follow God's Word and to believe in his power to save.

Leader: You remembered quite a bit.

Schooner: Treat people with love and respect, rejoice in God's care and give with a glad heart.

Leader: My, my, Schooner. I'm proud of you!

Schooner: Mighty *Moooooooooses.*

Leader: How I remember! Let's talk about the next leader. He name was Joshua.

Schooner: Mighty *Jooooooshuaaaa.*

Leader: Like Moses, he picked up his walking stick and led God's people through the desert.

Schooner: I don't need a walking stick, boss.

Leader: You don't?

Schooner: I don't walk much.

Leader: Oh, I suppose not.

Schooner: Birds like to fly.

Leader: Sounds like a faster way to travel.

Schooner: Hmm. Just think of it.

Leader: Yes?

Schooner: If God's people had wings they'd have cut their traveling time in half!

Leader: But…

Schooner: Then this Joshua fella could have hung up his sandals…

Leader: And…

Schooner: …and glided right in to the promised land.

Leader: Whoa! Back up a bit, Schooner.

Schooner: *(Schooner backs up a bit)*

Leader: *(shakes head)* God's chosen people, the Israelites, were people, not parrots.

Schooner: If you ask me, parrots would have made this whole travelin' thing a lot easier.

Leader: God isn't about easy, Schooner.

Schooner: No?

Leader: God is about using ordinary *people*, like Moses and Joshua to do amazing things.

Schooner: Like?

Leader: Talking to God face to face.

Schooner: *(nods in agreement)* That's amazing.

Leader: Like leading a community, millions of men and women, boys and girls, animals and wagons through the desert for 40 years.

Schooner: That sounds like a God thing, too, boss.

Leader: Until they came to their very own country, the promised land.

Schooner: God uses ordinary people to do amazing things.

Leader: When they serve God faithfully.

Schooner: God helping people. People helping people.

Leader: "For the Lord loves the just and will not forsake his faithful ones."

Schooner: You can't beat the Bible. Bible 4U! just around the bend.

1 Bible 4U!

Welcome to Bible 4U!—where the true stories of the Bible come to life in new and exciting ways! Today you'll need to tune your imagination to K-WOW TV as we watch a live broadcast from a point near the promised land. There is a rumor that the leadership of the Israelite nation is about to change. This is shocking in light of the fact that their current leader, Moses, has led these people for forty years.

Could it be that someone besides Moses will lead them home, into the promised land?

Instant Prep
Before class, choose four volunteers. You'll need solid readers for the Reporter and Woodrow. Peg and Rod have smaller parts. Give each volunteer a copy of the "A Wonderful Life" script below.

for Overachievers
Have a four person drama team prepare the story. Make signs for each character to identify his or her role. Wrap the Walking Stick family in burlap from their shoulders to their ankles. Dress the reporter in a khaki shirt and give him/her a microphone.

There is a sense of change in the air. The people are filled with anticipation. Moses has returned from one of his unique, face-to-face conversations with God. What is next for this mighty leader? Stay tuned for the inside scoop. Our reporter is with a family at the Israelite encampment not far from the Jordan River. Don't touch that remote—this will be a story to remember!

A Wonderful Life
Based on Numbers 27 and Deuteronomy 34

Reporter: This is a special report from K-WOW news. We're coming to you live from the Israelite camp. Moses, the long-time leader of the Israelite nation has returned from yet another encounter with the Lord. Joining us is the Walking Stick family. Woodrow, the eldest Walking Stick, has been with the Israelite people for many years. His grandchildren, Peg and Rod, have joined the Israelites in the last few months. Woodrow, what exactly does a walking stick do?

Woodrow: We give support and balance on a long hike. Our family slogan is quite catchy—"Lean On Me."

Reporter: How many years have you been in the business?

Woodrow: Almost forty. I belonged to one of the Israelite slaves who was set free from Egypt. He died a few years ago. Now I belong to his son.

Reporter: Aren't you getting a little, um, wobbly after all these years?

Woodrow: Nope. I'm stout as an oak. Probably a lot more sturdy than you will be when you have as many rings as I do.

Reporter: Er…uh…no offense, Woodrow. You look straight and strong to me.

Woodrow: My cousins were arrows.

Reporter: You must be very proud of them.

Woodrow: I am. But not nearly as proud as I am of these two little twiglets. As the Israelite nation has grown, we've needed new walking sticks to support new leaders.

Peg and Rod bow stiffly, then look at each other and giggle.

Reporter: Serving the Israelites appears to be a proud tradition that runs in the sap of your family tree.

Rod: You know, tree puns get a little old in our line of work.

Peg: Rod, you don't have to bark at him.

Reporter: Uh…right. Woodrow, is it true that Moses has spoken with God again?

Woodrow: Absolutely. No one else could do it, that's for sure.

Rod: I'd be petrified.

Peg: Hey! You were the one who was complaining about the tree puns.

Rod: Oops. I didn't do it on purpose.

Woodrow: Straighten up, you two. We're on live TV.

Reporter: Woodrow, what is the word Moses brought from God?

Woodrow: Well, seems Moses will not be entering the promised land with the rest of us. One time in the desert Moses didn't do exactly what God expected. God continued to bless him but told him he would not be able to enter the promised land.

Reporter: But Moses has been the leader of the Israelites for so many years. Who could ever fill his sandals?

Rod: That's easy! The leader of our army— Joshua. He's a great soldier.

Peg: *(sighs)* And he's handsome, too!

Woodrow: We all have confidence in Joshua. Moses brought him before the priest and commissioned him for the job. It was quite a moment when Moses laid his hands on Joshua.

Rod: I'd let him lean on me any day.

Reporter: I thought Moses was the one who did all the miracles. Will Joshua be able to pull those off?

Woodrow: You need to get your story straight, Mr. Reporter. God did the miracles. Moses is just a man who loves God and trusts him. God used him to do great things. Now God's blessing will rest on Joshua.

Rod: Yeah! Look out Canaanites—here comes Joshua!

Reporter: Who are the Canaanites?

Peg: The people who live in the promised land. It's going to be our land very soon.

Reporter: What about Moses? What happens to him now?

Woodrow: God is going to call him home. He is going to his rest.

Reporter: That will be a loss for your nation.

Woodrow: The people will mourn for him for thirty days. We'll remember how he led us. How he used his stick to part the sea and strike the rock to bring forth water.

Reporter: Those must have been great moments for you walking stick types.

Woodrow: We were glad to play a small role in the plans God had for his people.

Reporter: It's amazing what God can do with an ordinary stick. No offense.

Rod: Don't you see? God uses ordinary people, too.

Peg: But they have to be faithful people. People who love God more than anything else, and never give up!

Reporter: Is Joshua a faithful person?

Rod: You bet! He's strong and courageous.

Woodrow: I don't know if anyone will ever talk to God face-to-face as Moses did. But Joshua will be a fine leader.

Reporter: It sounds like Joshua can count on your support.

Peg: Always.

Everyone exits. Reporter returns.

Reporter: Evening has come to this peaceful valley. At the age of 120, Moses, faithful leader of the Israelites, has seen his last day. It's reported that he spent his last hours viewing the promised land from a mountain-top, seeing the future of the nation in the company of the Lord that he so faithfully loved and served. There will never be another prophet in all of Israel like Moses, but he dies today knowing that the nation is safe in the hands of Joshua.

Moses had a wonderful life chockful of fear and faith, hardship and adventure. How much of his biography do you remember?

Toss the four numbered balls to different parts of the room. Bring the kids with the balls to the front one-by-one and ask these questions. Allow kids to get help from the group if they need it. After each correct answer, let kids drop the ball into a bag.

 ■ **What happened when Moses was a baby?**

 ■ **What did Moses do that no one else had ever done?** *(Talked to God face to face.)*

 ■ **What made Moses so special?**

 ■ **What's one thing you've learned from Moses' life?**

Moses' life was like the greatest adventure film you've ever seen. Only none of it was special effects. It was all real, done by the hand of God. Plagues, a sea that parted, fire and smoke on the mountain where he met God, the Ten Commandments on tablets of stone, just to name a few highlights. This was the man God chose to free his people from slavery in Egypt and guide them through the desert until they came to the promised land. You can imagine how difficult it must have been for the Israelites to say goodbye to him.

Bible Verse
For the Lord loves the just and will not forsake his faithful ones.
Psalms 37:28

There's one important thing I want you to remember from these stories about Moses: he was faithful to God. When going back to Egypt to face Pharaoh was the last thing in the world he wanted to do, he did it because God told him to. He trusted God in the face of terrifying armies and hungry, thirsty people. And God never failed him.

God still needs faithful people—ordinary people like you and me who will do his work in the world. You may not be a prince of Egypt, but if you trust God he will use you.

Dismiss kids to their shepherd groups.

2 Shepherd's Spot

Gather kids in your small group and help them find Deuteronomy 34 in their Bibles. Ask a volunteer to read verses 1–11 out loud.

Wow. After all these years and all the wonderful things he's done, Moses went up on a mountaintop and died and God buried him.

- **What do you remember about Moses' life?**
- **If you could drop in to any of these stories and live beside Moses, which story would you choose?**

Moses did amazing things, but it was God who gave him the power to do all those miracles. Why did God pick Moses? Maybe God knew that Moses loved him more than anything, and that because of that love, he would be faithful no matter what. God has always used faithful people to build his kingdom here on earth.

- **Can you think of some faithful people who have touched your life?**

God's people honored Moses, and we want to honor faithful leaders who have pointed us toward God. Here's a fun card you can make and share with someone who's been an important leader for you.

Distribute the "Love That Leader!" handout (p. 124). Lead kids through the assembly instructions on the card. Let kids decorate it with art supplies you have on hand. Encourage them to write a small personal note to the leader who will receive their cards.

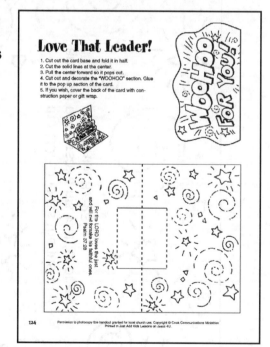

Love That Leader!

1. Cut out the card base and fold it in half.
2. Cut the solid lines at the center.
3. Pull the center forward so it pops out.
4. Cut out and decorate the "WOOHOO" section. Glue it to the pop up up section of the card.
5. If you wish, cover the back of the card with construction paper or gift wrap.

For the LORD loves the just and will not forsake his faithful ones. Psalm 37:28

124   Permission to photocopy this handout granted for local church use. Copyright © Cook Communications Ministries   Printed in Just Add Kids Lessons on Jesus 4U.

These look really great! Can you imagine how delighted people will be to receive them? Let's pray for leaders who are important to us. When I pause, add the name of the person who will receive your card. Heavenly father, thank you for the wonderful people you bring into our lives who help us know you better. We thank you especially for *(pause for kids to respond).* **We ask your special blessing and encouragement for each one of these people. Help us grow to be like them. In Jesus' name, amen.**

Love That Leader!

1. Cut out the card base and fold it in half.
2. Cut the solid lines at the center.
3. Pull the center forward so it pops out.
4. Cut out and decorate the "WOOHOO" section. Glue it to the pop-up section of the card.
5. If you wish, cover the back of the card with construction paper or gift wrap.

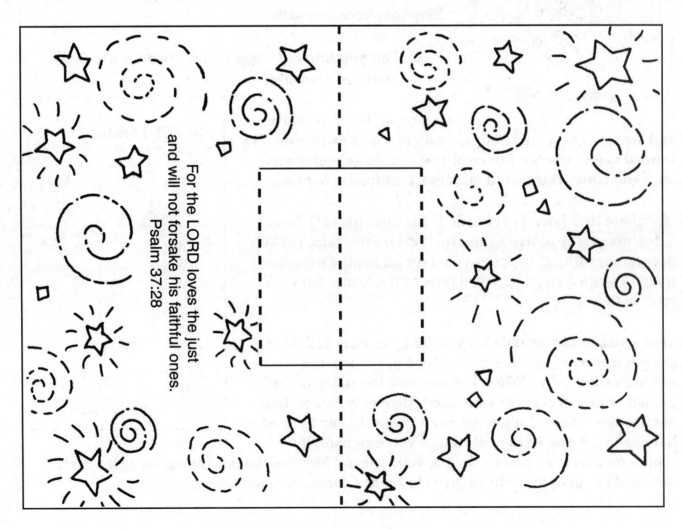

For the LORD loves the just and will not forsake his faithful ones.
Psalm 37:28

Use tree branches to make kid-size walking sticks. If tree branches are not available use wrapping paper tubes instead. There's no need to remove the wrapping paper or the outer plastic covering. Kids can wrap twine (as explained below) and/or tape and glue lightweight items to the plastic to personalize their sticks.

Get List:
- ☐ dry, sturdy tree branches
- ☐ fine sandpaper
- ☐ acrylic paints and brushes
- ☐ twine

Optional:
- ☐ wrapping paper rolls
- ☐ feathers
- ☐ pinecones
- ☐ beads
- ☐ ribbons

When God showed Moses the land he planned to give his people, Moses was also told that he would not be the leader to get them there. Another "ordinary" man by the name of Joshua would take God's people to the promised land. From this day forward, the Israelite nation followed the strong leader Joshua.

■ **If you took a hike, what kind of adventure would you choose?**
   a) beginner b) intermediate c) 40-year trek

■ **What would keep you from getting lost on your journey?** *(Listening to the leader and faithfully trusting his steps).*

So the journey was not yet over for God's people. They needed to keep in step and remain faithful followers. With walking sticks in hand they traveled on. Walking sticks were used by many of the Israelites to aid them on their journey. They were used not only for support in climbing hills, crossing deserts or traveling over rocky soil, but for beating the bushes and low brushwood for the snakes and other reptiles that posed a constant threat for travelers. And, of course, when the traveler became weary, the support of the stick was very much appreciated.

Select sturdy, dry branches. The key is to find one that fits the student comfortably. Generally, it should be chest high and easy to grip. Peel away the loose bark by hand. Smooth the rough spots with fine sandpaper.

When the stick feels comfortable to the student, it is ready to decorate. Paint bright and bold patterns onto the stick. **Like you, the Israelites loved color!** When the paint is dry, wrap some twine and knot both ends. Tie or glue on items of the student's choosing (feathers, pinecones, yarn, beads, stickers, ribbons, jewels, etc.). Make sure to leave the top of the sticks clear of objects that would get in the way of a sturdy grip.

Simpler Option: Forgo the paints, which require drying time. Instead, take the students on a short walk outside. Ask them to visualize a group traveling together.

Now you have a walking stick like the one used so many years ago by the Israelite children. Use it as you leave today as a reminder to serve God faithfully as Joshua did in today's story. If necessary, remind your kids that walking sticks are just that—used for walking. They should not be used as swords or poking implements.

Fold down the corners to start your paper airplane.

SPECIAL DELIVERY

TO

Serve God faithfully.

Do you feel ordinary, just like everybody else? Name two ordinary people from the Bible that God used to carry out his plan. (Noah, Jonah, Moses, Joshua, Joseph, Mary, the disciples!)

How did Joshua serve God faithfully in today's story?

Today at church we learned that Moses passed leadership to Joshua.

Family FUN

Take ordinary piecrust dough and pass it on—like Moses passed on leadership of God's people to Joshua in today's story. Ask Mom or Dad's help in mixing up a batch of pie crust dough. Flour your hands and break off a small piece. Flatten it into a dough circle—then pass it on to Mom or Dad. Have your helper fold the dough in half and use a knife to cut out triangles on the fold. Pass it on again! Open the dough and refold to cut even more shapes. Sprinkle with cinnamon and sugar and bake at 425° until lightly browned.

Bible Verse

For the LORD loves the just and will not forsake his faithful ones.
Psalm 37:28

Live It!

◇ How can faithful obedience to God produce amazing results?

◇ Can you name one simple way you serve God faithfully during the week?